Lectio Divina

of the

Gospels

for the Liturgical Year

2022-2023

UNITED STATES CONFERENCE OF CATHOLIC BISHOPS

WASHINGTON, DC

Contents

Reading seeks for the sweetness of a blessed life,
meditation perceives it,
prayer asks for it,
contemplation tastes it.

Reading, as it were, puts food whole into the mouth,
meditation chews it and breaks it up,
prayer extracts its flavor,
contemplation is the sweetness itself
which gladdens and refreshes.

Reading works on the outside,
meditation on the pith,
prayer asks for what we long for,
contemplation gives us delight in the sweetness
which we have found.

—Guigo II, *The Ladder of Monks*, III (12th c.)

What Is *Lectio Divina* and How to Use This Book

Reading – Meditation – Prayer – Contemplation

Lectio divina or "divine reading" is a process of engaging with Christ, the Word of God. Through this sacred exercise, we enter into a closer relationship with the very Word himself, who communicates the love of the Father to us through the Holy Spirit.

Lectio divina has four steps in which we first hear what God has said (reading). We then take it in and reflect on it (meditation). From this our hearts are lifted up (prayer). Finally, after speaking to the Lord in prayer, we rest and listen for his message to us (contemplation).

This is the process of *lectio divina*. It is a conversation with God, grounded in God's own self-revelation to us. This helps us speak to God with a focus on what he has already told us about his relationship with humanity, his plans and desires for us, his promises, his admonitions, and his guidance on how we can live, so as to find true life in abundance in Christ.

Here is a brief description of each of the four steps:

Reading (*Lectio*)

Read the passage slowly and allow it to sink in.

If there is a passage that is particularly striking, and that you want to keep with you, consider committing it to memory, or writing it down to keep with you, so that you can re-read it throughout the day, and let it enter deeper into your spirit.

"Faith comes from what is heard, and what is heard comes through the word of Christ." (Romans 10:17)

"The word of God is living and effective, sharper than any two-edged sword, penetrating even between soul and spirit, joints and marrow, and able to discern reflections and thoughts of the heart." (Hebrews 4:12)

Meditation (*Meditatio*)

Read the passage again, and when something strikes you, a question arises in you, stop and meditate. Think about what God may be saying through it.

"It is the glory of God to conceal a matter,
  and the glory of kings to fathom a matter."
(Proverbs 25:2)

"I will ponder your precepts and consider your paths."
(Psalm 119:15)

Prayer (*Oratio*)

Speak to the Lord about what you have read and share what's on your mind and heart—offer and share with the Lord your thanksgiving, petition, concerns, doubts, or simply affirm, back to the Lord, the very word that he has spoken.

"Enter his gates with thanksgiving,
   his courts with praise."
(Psalm 100:4)

"Ask and it will be given to you; seek and you will find; knock and the door will be opened to you." (Matthew 7:7)

Contemplation (*Contemplatio*)

This is a quiet time, a time to rest in his presence and wait upon the Lord. It is a time where we allow the Lord to speak directly to our spirit from within us. It requires practice. But this allows us to be attentive to the Lord's voice, and by regular practice, our ability to hear God's voice will grow in daily life and daily situations, as we learn to focus our minds and hearts, our thoughts, our concerns, and our hopes toward him.

"My sheep hear my voice; I know them, and they follow me." (John 10:27)

"Be still and know that I am God!" (Psalm 46:11)

Applying This Process of *Lectio Divina* to the Liturgical Year

This *Lectio Divina of the Gospels for the Liturgical Year* book will take the reader through the Sundays and major feasts and solemnities of the liturgical year. It can be used for individual devotion and can also easily be used to assist in small group reflections in parishes and small faith groups. It offers a structured process for engaging with the Word of God. As the reader or group becomes more comfortable engaging with Scripture, this process can be more closely tailored to suit the path of growth that best fits the reader(s).

First, the *lectio divina* session is started by praying a prayer that is taken from a Mass collect from that liturgical week. Following that prayer, the main scripture passage for reflection is read, which is taken from the gospel reading for that day. This READING can be re-read, a few times, to let it sink in. Next, a set of three questions are offered to help in MEDITATION. These questions can also facilitate talking about the passage in a group setting. The individual then offers his or her personal PRAYER, responding to the Lord. In a group setting, people can speak out their prayers one at a time—this may help deepen the prayer response and further set the group's focus on the Lord.

Next, a structured set of passages and questions are offered that return the reader back to the gospel passage. This invites the reader to contemplate what the Lord is speaking and what it means for their life. It allows the individual or the prayer group to consider specific ways the Lord may be speaking into their life at that very moment. As each person begins to hear a response from the Lord—the Lord's word spoken directly and personally to them—that person can begin let that word flow through their life, by an interior change and a will to do what the Lord is asking of them. Through this step of CONTEMPLATION, we hear God's voice speaking to us, and it propels us to conversion of heart and mind.

After the closing prayer, time is given to choosing how to live out the fruit of your prayer. You know your heart and life best—if it's clear what God is asking of you, in faith, choose some way that you can put that request or teaching from the Lord into action that week. It could be a small act of faith that the Lord is asking, or perhaps, a more serious and important step that he is asking you to take. If there is nothing specific that comes to your mind, consider the question and suggestion offered in the *Living the Word This Week* section. This portion offers guidance on what concrete actions may be taken in our daily lives.

The *Lectio Divina of the Gospels for the Liturgical Year* offers a specific pattern of prayerful reading of God's Word. As you begin on this path, may the Lord's blessing follow you, and fall upon you, throughout the movement of seasons in this new liturgical year, and may your life, in turn, be a blessing upon others.

Lectio
Divina
of the
Gospels

November 27, 2022

Lectio Divina for the First Sunday of Advent

We begin our prayer:

In the name of the Father, and of the Son, and of the Holy Spirit. Amen.

Keep us alert, we pray, O Lord our God,
as we await the advent of Chrtist your Son,
so that, when he comes and knocks,
he may find us watchful in prayer
and exultant in his praise.
Who lives and reigns with you in the unity of the Holy Spirit,
God, for ever and ever.

Collect, Monday of the First Week of Advent

Reading (*Lectio*)

Read the following Scripture two or three times.

Matthew 24:37-44

> Jesus said to his disciples: "As it was in the days of Noah, so it will be at the coming of the Son of Man. In those days before the flood, they were eating and drinking, marrying and giving in marriage, up to the day that Noah entered the ark. They did not know until the flood came and carried them all away. So will it be also at the coming of the Son of Man. Two men will be out in the field; one will be taken, and one will be left. Two women will be grinding at the mill; one will be taken, and one will be left. Therefore, stay awake! For you do not know on which day your Lord will come. Be sure of this: if the master of the house had known the hour of night when the thief was coming, he would have stayed awake and not let his house be broken into. So too, you also must be prepared, for at an hour you do not expect, the Son of Man will come."

Meditation (*Meditatio*)

After the reading, take some time to reflect in silence on one or more of the following questions:

- What word or words in this passage caught your attention?
- What in this passage comforted you?
- What in this passage challenged you?

If practicing lectio divina *as a family or in a group, after the reflection time, invite the participants to share their responses.*

Prayer (*Oratio*)

Read the scripture passage one more time. Bring to the Lord the praise, petition, or thanksgiving that the Word inspires in you.

Contemplation (*Contemplatio*)

Read the Scripture again, followed by this reflection:

∼ What conversion of mind, heart, and life is the Lord asking of me?

_____

_____

_____

_____

∼ *In those days before the flood, they were eating and drinking, marrying and giving in marriage, up to the day that Noah entered the ark.* How can I make more time for God in the busyness of daily life? How can I become more attentive to the presence of God in the everyday aspects of my life?

_____

_____

_____

_____

≈ *So will it be also at the coming of the Son of Man.* How can I prepare my heart to be a worthy home for the Lord? How can I grow in longing for the coming of the Lord?

_____

_____

_____

_____

≈ *One will be taken, and one will be left.* When have I felt left out or forgotten? How can learn to notice and reach out to those on the margins?

_____

_____

_____

_____

≈ *After a period of silent reflection and/or discussion, all recite the Lord's Prayer and the following:*

Closing Prayer

I rejoiced because they said to me,
  "We will go up to the house of the LORD."
And now we have set foot
  within your gates, O Jerusalem.

Jerusalem, built as a city
    with compact unity.
To it the tribes go up,
    the tribes of the LORD.

According to the decree for Israel,
    to give thanks to the name of the LORD.
In it are set up judgment seats,
    seats for the house of David.

Pray for the peace of Jerusalem!
    May those who love you prosper!
May peace be within your walls,
    prosperity in your buildings.

Because of my brothers and friends
    I will say, "Peace be within you!"
Because of the house of the LORD, our God,
    I will pray for your good.

From Psalm 122

Living the Word This Week

How can I make my life a gift for others in charity?

Choose a spiritual or corporal work of mercy to practice this Advent to prepare your heart for Christ's coming.

December 4, 2022

Lectio Divina for the Second Week of Advent

We begin our prayer:

In the name of the Father, and of the Son, and of the Holy Spirit. Amen.

Stir up our hearts, O Lord,
to make ready the paths
of your Only Begotten Son,
that through his coming,
we may be found worthy to serve you
with minds made pure.
Through our Lord Jesus Christ, your Son,
who lives and reigns with you in the unity of the Holy Spirit,
God, for ever and ever.

Collect, Thursday of the Second Week of Advent

Reading (*Lectio*)

Read the following Scripture two or three times.

Matthew 3:1-12

John the Baptist appeared, preaching in the desert of Judea and saying, "Repent, for the kingdom of heaven is at hand!" It was of him that the prophet Isaiah had spoken when he said:

A voice of one crying out in the desert,
Prepare the way of the Lord,
*   make straight his paths.*

John wore clothing made of camel's hair and had a leather belt around his waist. His food was locusts and wild honey. At that time Jerusalem, all Judea, and the whole region around the Jordan were going out to him and were being baptized by him in the Jordan River as they acknowledged their sins.

When he saw many of the Pharisees and Sadducees coming to his baptism, he said to them, "You brood of vipers! Who warned you to flee from the coming wrath? Produce good fruit as evidence of your repentance. And do not presume to say to yourselves, 'We have Abraham as our father.' For I tell you, God can raise up children to Abraham from these stones. Even now the ax lies at the root of the trees. Therefore every tree that does not bear good fruit will be cut down and thrown into the fire. I am baptizing you with water, for repentance, but the one who is coming after me is mightier than I. I am not worthy to carry his sandals. He will baptize you with the Holy Spirit and fire. His winnowing fan is in his hand. He will clear his threshing floor and gather his wheat into his barn, but the chaff he will burn with unquenchable fire."

Meditation (*Meditatio*)

After the reading, take some time to reflect in silence on one or more of the following questions:

- What word or words in this passage caught your attention?
- What in this passage comforted you?
- What in this passage challenged you?

If practicing lectio divina *as a family or in a group, after the reflection time, invite the participants to share their responses.*

Prayer (*Oratio*)

Read the scripture passage one more time. Bring to the Lord the praise, petition, or thanksgiving that the Word inspires in you.

Contemplation (*Contemplatio*)

Read the Scripture again, followed by this reflection:

≈ What conversion of mind, heart, and life is the Lord asking of me?

_____

_____

_____

_____

≈ *A voice of one crying out in the desert,/ Prepare the way of the Lord,/ make straight his paths.* When have I felt like a voice crying out in the desert? When have I failed to use my voice when I should have?

_____

_____

_____

_____

≈ *The whole region around the Jordan ... were being baptized by him in the Jordan River as they acknowledged their sins.* What sins am I struggling with today? What prevents me from acknowledging my sinfulness and relying on God's mercy?

_____

_____

_____

_____

≈ *I am not worthy to carry his sandals.* How can I serve the Lord? How can I grow in humility and docility to the Lord's will?

_____

_____

_____

_____

Closing Prayer

I will hear what God proclaims;
    The LORD —for he proclaims peace to his people.
Near indeed is his salvation to those who fear him,
    glory dwelling in our land.

Kindness and truth shall meet;
    justice and peace shall kiss.
Truth shall spring out of the earth,
    and justice shall look down from heaven.

The LORD himself will give his benefits;
    our land shall yield its increase.
Justice shall walk before him,
    and prepare the way of his steps.

From Psalm 72

Living the Word This Week

How can I make my life a gift for others in charity?

Make plans to receive the Sacrament of Penance this Advent.

December 8, 2022

Lectio Divina for the Solemnity of the Immaculate Conception

We begin our prayer:

In the name of the Father, and of the Son, and of the Holy Spirit. Amen.

O God, who by the Immaculate Conception of the Blessed Virgin
prepared a worthy dwelling for your Son,
grant, we pray,
that, as you preserved her from every stain
by virtue of the Death of your Son, which you foresaw,
so, through her intercession,
we, too, may be cleansed and admitted to your presence.
Through our Lord Jesus Christ, your Son,
who lives and reigns with you in the unity of the Holy Spirit,
God, for ever and ever.

Collect, Solemnity of the Immaculate Conception

Reading (*Lectio*)

Read the following Scripture two or three times.

Luke 1:26-38

> The angel Gabriel was sent from God to a town of Galilee called Nazareth, to a virgin betrothed to a man named Joseph, of the house of David, and the virgin's name was Mary. And coming to her, he said, "Hail, full of grace! The Lord is with you." But she was greatly troubled at what was said and pondered what sort of greeting this might be. Then the angel said to her, "Do not be afraid, Mary, for you have found favor with God. Behold, you will conceive in your womb and bear a son, and you shall name him Jesus. He will be great and will be called Son of the Most High, and the Lord God will give him the throne of David his father, and he will rule over the house of Jacob forever, and of his Kingdom there will be no end." But Mary said to the angel, "How can this be, since I have no relations with a man?" And the angel said to her in reply, "The Holy Spirit will come upon you, and the power of the Most High will overshadow you. Therefore the child to be born will be called holy, the Son of God. And behold, Elizabeth, your relative, has also conceived a son in her old age, and this is the sixth month for her who was called barren; for nothing will be impossible for God." Mary said, "Behold, I am the handmaid of the Lord. May it be done to me according to your word." Then the angel departed from her.

Meditation (*Meditatio*)

After the reading, take some time to reflect in silence on one or more of the following questions:

- What word or words in this passage caught your attention?
- What in this passage comforted you?
- What in this passage challenged you?

If practicing lectio divina *as a family or in a group, after the reflection time, invite the participants to share their responses.*

Prayer (*Oratio*)

Read the scripture passage one more time. Bring to the Lord the praise, petition, or thanksgiving that the Word inspires in you.

Contemplation (*Contemplatio*)

Read the Scripture again, followed by this reflection:

≈ What conversion of mind, heart, and life is the Lord asking of me?

_____

_____

_____

_____

≈ *"Hail, full of grace! The Lord is with you."* When have I felt the grace and favor of God most strongly? How can I become more attuned to the gift of God's grace in my life?

_____

_____

_____

_____

❧ *But she was greatly troubled at what was said and pondered what sort of greeting this might be.* When have I felt anxious or unsure about my faith? How can the Church and her perennial teaching strengthen and confirm my faith?

_____

_____

_____

_____

❧ *Do not be afraid.* What fears keep me from serving God more wholeheartedly? How can I offer comfort and assurance to those around me?

_____

_____

_____

_____

❧ *After a period of silent reflection and/or discussion, all recite the Lord's Prayer and the following:*

Closing Prayer

Sing to the LORD a new song,
 for he has done wondrous deeds;
His right hand has won victory for him,
 his holy arm.

The LORD has made his salvation known:
 in the sight of the nations he has revealed his justice.
He has remembered his kindness and his faithfulness
 toward the house of Israel.

All the ends of the earth have seen
 the salvation by our God.
Sing joyfully to the LORD, all you lands;
 break into song; sing praise.

From Psalm 98

Living the Word This Week

How can I make my life a gift for others in charity?

Pray a Rosary for those in the Church who are called to teach and strengthen the faith.

December 11, 2022

Lectio Divina for the Third Week of Advent

We begin our prayer:

In the name of the Father, and of the Son, and of the Holy Spirit. Amen.

Incline a merciful ear to our cry, we pray, O Lord,
and, casting light on the darkness of our hearts,
visit us with the grace of your Son.
Who lives and reigns with you in the unity of the Holy Spirit,
God, for ever and ever.

Collect, Monday of the Third Week of Advent

Reading (*Lectio*)

Read the following Scripture two or three times.

Matthew 11:2-11

When John the Baptist heard in prison of the works of the Christ,
he sent his disciples to Jesus with this question, "Are you the one
who is to come, or should we look for another?" Jesus said to them
in reply, "Go and tell John what you hear and see: the blind regain

their sight, the lame walk, lepers are cleansed, the deaf hear, the dead are raised, and the poor have the good news proclaimed to them. And blessed is the one who takes no offense at me."

As they were going off, Jesus began to speak to the crowds about John, "What did you go out to the desert to see? A reed swayed by the wind? Then what did you go out to see? Someone dressed in fine clothing? Those who wear fine clothing are in royal palaces. Then why did you go out? To see a prophet? Yes, I tell you, and more than a prophet. This is the one about whom it is written:

Behold, I am sending my messenger ahead of you;
he will prepare your way before you.

Amen, I say to you, among those born of women there has been none greater than John the Baptist; yet the least in the kingdom of heaven is greater than he."

Meditation (*Meditatio*)

After the reading, take some time to reflect in silence on one or more of the following questions:

- What word or words in this passage caught your attention?
- What in this passage comforted you?
- What in this passage challenged you?

If practicing lectio divina *as a family or in a group, after the reflection time, invite the participants to share their responses.*

Prayer (*Oratio*)

Read the scripture passage one more time. Bring to the Lord the praise, petition, or thanksgiving that the Word inspires in you.

Contemplation (*Contemplatio*)

Read the Scripture again, followed by this reflection:

≈ What conversion of mind, heart, and life is the Lord asking of me?

_____

_____

_____

_____

≈ *"Are you the one who is to come, or should we look for another?"* What people, events, or things distract me from God? How can I be more aware of God's presence?

_____

_____

_____

_____

～ *Go and tell John what you hear and see.* How have I shared my faith with those I meet? How do my words and actions proclaim the good news?

_____

_____

_____

_____

～ *He will prepare your way before you.* How can I help to prepare the Lord's way? How can I make my heart ready to receive the Lord?

_____

_____

_____

_____

～ *After a period of silent reflection and/or discussion, all recite the Lord's Prayer and the following:*

Closing Prayer

The LORD God keeps faith forever,
    secures justice for the oppressed,
    gives food to the hungry.
The LORD sets captives free.

The LORD gives sight to the blind;
>   the LORD raises up those who were bowed down.
The LORD loves the just;
>   the LORD protects strangers.

The fatherless and the widow he sustains,
>   but the way of the wicked he thwarts.
The LORD shall reign forever;
>   your God, O Zion, through all generations.

From Psalm 146

Living the Word This Week

How can I make my life a gift for others in charity?

In this season of giving, donate your time, treasure, or talent to those in need.

December 18, 2022

Lectio Divina for the Fourth Week of Advent

We begin our prayer:

In the name of the Father, and of the Son, and of the Holy Spirit. Amen.

Come quickly, we pray, Lord Jesus,
and do not delay,
that those who trust in your compassion
may find solace and relief in your coming.
Who live and reign with God the Father
in the unity of the Holy Spirit,
God, for ever and ever.

Collect, December 23

Reading (*Lectio*)

Read the following Scripture two or three times.

Matthew 1:18-24

This is how the birth of Jesus Christ came about. When his mother Mary was betrothed to Joseph, but before they lived together, she was found with child through the Holy Spirit. Joseph her husband, since he was a righteous man, yet unwilling to expose her to shame, decided to divorce her quietly. Such was his intention when, behold, the angel of the Lord appeared to him in a dream and said, "Joseph, son of David, do not be afraid to take Mary your wife into your home. For it is through the Holy Spirit that this child has been conceived in her. She will bear a son and you are to name him Jesus, because he will save his people from their sins." All this took place to fulfill what the Lord had said through the prophet:

Behold, the virgin shall conceive and bear a son,
    and they shall name him Emmanuel,

which means "God is with us." When Joseph awoke, he did as the angel of the Lord had commanded him and took his wife into his home.

Meditation (*Meditatio*)

After the reading, take some time to reflect in silence on one or more of the following questions:

- What word or words in this passage caught your attention?
- What in this passage comforted you?
- What in this passage challenged you?

If practicing lectio divina *as a family or in a group, after the reflection time, invite the participants to share their responses.*

Prayer (*Oratio*)

Read the scripture passage one more time. Bring to the Lord the praise, petition, or thanksgiving that the Word inspires in you.

Contemplation (*Contemplatio*)

Read the Scripture again, followed by this reflection:

≈ What conversion of mind, heart, and life is the Lord asking of me?

_____

_____

_____

_____

≈ *He was a righteous man, yet unwilling to expose her to shame.* When have my actions shamed and hurt people rather than supported them? Who in my life is in need of extra care these days?

_____

_____

_____

_____

≈ *Such was his intention when, behold, the angel of the Lord appeared to him in a dream.* How have I heard God speaking to me? How have I responded to God's voice?

_____

_____

_____

_____

≈ *"God is with us."* When have I felt God's presence most strongly? How can I become more aware of God's presence in my life?

_____

_____

_____

_____

≈ *After a period of silent reflection and/or discussion, all recite the Lord's Prayer and the following:*

Closing Prayer

The LORD's are the earth and its fullness;
    the world and those who dwell in it.
For he founded it upon the seas
    and established it upon the rivers.

Who can ascend the mountain of the LORD?
 or who may stand in his holy place?
One whose hands are sinless, whose heart is clean,
 who desires not what is vain.

He shall receive a blessing from the LORD,
 a reward from God his savior.
Such is the race that seeks for him,
 that seeks the face of the God of Jacob.

From Psalm 24

Living the Word This Week

How can I make my life a gift for others in charity?

Learn how you can help your parish or diocese Walk with Moms in Need: https://walkingwithmoms.com.

December 25, 2022

Lectio Divina for the Solemnity of Christmas

We begin our prayer:

In the name of the Father, and of the Son, and of the Holy Spirit. Amen.

O God, who wonderfully created the dignity of human nature
and still more wonderfully restored it,
grant, we pray,
that we may share in the divinity of Christ,
who humbled himself to share in our humanity.
Who lives and reigns with you in the unity of the Holy Spirit,
God, for ever and ever.

Collect, Christmas, Mass during the Day

Reading (*Lectio*)

Read the following Scripture two or three times.

John 1:1-5, 9-14

In the beginning was the Word,
    and the Word was with God,
    and the Word was God.
He was in the beginning with God.
All things came to be through him,
    and without him nothing came to be.
What came to be through him was life,
    and this life was the light of the human race;
the light shines in the darkness,
    and the darkness has not overcome it.

The true light, which enlightens everyone, was coming into the world.

He was in the world,
    and the world came to be through him,
    but the world did not know him.
He came to what was his own,
    but his own people did not accept him.

But to those who did accept him
    he gave power to become children of God,
    to those who believe in his name,
    who were born not by natural generation
    nor by human choice nor by a man's decision
    but of God.

And the Word became flesh
and made his dwelling among us,
and we saw his glory,
the glory as of the Father's only Son,
full of grace and truth.

Meditation (*Meditatio*)

After the reading, take some time to reflect in silence on one or more of the following questions:

- What word or words in this passage caught your attention?
- What in this passage comforted you?
- What in this passage challenged you?

If practicing lectio divina *as a family or in a group, after the reflection time, invite the participants to share their responses.*

Prayer (*Oratio*)

Read the scripture passage one more time. Bring to the Lord the praise, petition, or thanksgiving that the Word inspires in you.

Contemplation (*Contemplatio*)

Read the Scripture again, followed by this reflection:

∾ What conversion of mind, heart, and life is the Lord asking of me?

_____

_____

_____

_____

≈ *The light shines in the darkness,/ and the darkness has not overcome it.* What steps can I take to overcome sin and evil in my life? How can I share the light and warmth of God's love and truth?

_____

_____

_____

_____

≈ *He was in the world,/ and the world came to be through him.* How do I experience the presence of God through creation? What life changes can I make to better protect our common home?

_____

_____

_____

_____

≈ *And the Word became flesh/ and made his dwelling among us.* How can I grow in love of God's holy Word? How can I grow in love and closeness to the Lord?

_____

_____

_____

_____

≈ *After a period of silent reflection and/or discussion, all recite the Lord's Prayer and the following:*

Closing Prayer

Sing to the LORD a new song,
> for he has done wondrous deeds;
his right hand has won victory for him,
> his holy arm.

The LORD has made his salvation known:
> in the sight of the nations he has revealed his justice.
He has remembered his kindness and his faithfulness
> oward the house of Israel.

All the ends of the earth have seen
> the salvation by our God.
Sing joyfully to the LORD, all you lands;
> break into song; sing praise.

Sing praise to the LORD with the harp,
    with the harp and melodious song.
With trumpets and the sound of the horn
    sing joyfully before the King, the LORD.

From Psalm 98

Living the Word This Week

How can I make my life a gift for others in charity?

Make a resolution to pray with Scripture every week.

January 1, 2023

Lectio Divina for the Solemnity of Mary, Mother of God

We begin our prayer:

In the name of the Father, and of the Son, and of the Holy Spirit. Amen.

O God, who through the fruitful virginity of Blessed Mary
bestowed on the human race
the grace of eternal salvation,
grant, we pray,
that we may experience the intercession of her,
through whom we were found worthy
to receive the author of life,
our Lord Jesus Christ, your Son.
Who lives and reigns with you in the unity of the Holy Spirit,
God, for ever and ever.

Collect, Solemnity of Mary, Mother of God

Reading (*Lectio*)

Read the following Scripture two or three times.

Luke 2:16-21

> The shepherds went in haste to Bethlehem and found Mary and Joseph, and the infant lying in the manger. When they saw this, they made known the message that had been told them about this child. All who heard it were amazed by what had been told them by the shepherds. And Mary kept all these things, reflecting on them in her heart. Then the shepherds returned, glorifying and praising God for all they had heard and seen, just as it had been told to them.
>
> When eight days were completed for his circumcision, he was named Jesus, the name given him by the angel before he was conceived in the womb.

Meditation (*Meditatio*)

After the reading, take some time to reflect in silence on one or more of the following questions:

- What word or words in this passage caught your attention?
- What in this passage comforted you?
- What in this passage challenged you?

If practicing lectio divina *as a family or in a group, after the reflection time, invite the participants to share their responses.*

Prayer (*Oratio*)

Read the scripture passage one more time. Bring to the Lord the praise, petition, or thanksgiving that the Word inspires in you.

Contemplation (*Contemplatio*)

Read the Scripture again, followed by this reflection:

≈ What conversion of mind, heart, and life is the Lord asking of me?

_____

_____

_____

_____

≈ *The shepherds went in haste to Bethlehem.* Where is God calling me to go? How can I hasten to do God's will?

_____

_____

_____

_____

≈ *All who heard it were amazed by what had been told them by the shepherds.* How can I let amazement break through my cynicism and weariness? When have God's actions aroused my sense of wonder and awe?

_____

_____

_____

_____

≈ *Mary kept all these things, reflecting on them in her heart.* What time do I dedicate to prayer and reflection? What do I need to tune out in order to focus on God?

_____

_____

_____

_____

≈ *After a period of silent reflection and/or discussion, all recite the Lord's Prayer and the following:*

Closing Prayer

May God have pity on us and bless us;
 may he let his face shine upon us.
So may your way be known upon earth;
 among all nations, your salvation.

May the nations be glad and exult
 because you rule the peoples in equity;
 the nations on the earth you guide.

May the peoples praise you, O God;
 may all the peoples praise you!
May God bless us,
 and may all the ends of the earth fear him

From Psalm 67

Living the Word This Week

How can I make my life a gift for others in charity?

Before bed each night, reflect on how God was present to you during the day and give God thanks and praise for this gift.

January 8, 2023

Lectio Divina for the Solemnity of the Epiphany

We begin our prayer:

In the name of the Father, and of the Son, and of the Holy Spirit. Amen.

May the splendor of your majesty, O Lord, we pray,
shed its light upon our hearts,
that we may pass through the shadows of this world
and reach the brightness of our eternal home.
Through our Lord Jesus Christ, your Son,
who lives and reigns with you in the unity of the Holy Spirit,
God, for ever and ever.

Collect, Solemnity of the Epiphany, Vigil Mass

Reading (*Lectio*)

Read the following Scripture two or three times.

Matthew 2:1-12

When Jesus was born in Bethlehem of Judea, in the days of King Herod, behold, magi from the east arrived in Jerusalem, saying, "Where is the newborn king of the Jews? We saw his star at its rising and have come to do him homage." When King Herod heard this, he was greatly troubled, and all Jerusalem with him. Assembling all the chief priests and the scribes of the people, he inquired of them where the Christ was to be born. They said to him, "In Bethlehem of Judea, for thus it has been written through the prophet:

And you, Bethlehem, land of Judah,
*   are by no means least among the rulers of Judah;*
since from you shall come a ruler,
*   who is to shepherd my people Israel."*

Then Herod called the magi secretly and ascertained from them the time of the star's appearance. He sent them to Bethlehem and said, "Go and search diligently for the child. When you have found him, bring me word, that I too may go and do him homage." After their audience with the king they set out. And behold, the star that they had seen at its rising preceded them, until it came and stopped over the place where the child was. They were overjoyed at seeing the star, and on entering the house they saw the child with Mary his mother. They prostrated themselves and did him homage. Then they opened their treasures and offered him gifts of gold, frankincense, and myrrh. And having been warned in a dream not to return to Herod, they departed for their country by another way.

Meditation (*Meditatio*)

After the reading, take some time to reflect in silence on one or more of the following questions:

- What word or words in this passage caught your attention?
- What in this passage comforted you?
- What in this passage challenged you?

If practicing lectio divina *as a family or in a group, after the reflection time, invite the participants to share their responses.*

Prayer (*Oratio*)

Read the scripture passage one more time. Bring to the Lord the praise, petition, or thanksgiving that the Word inspires in you.

Contemplation (*Contemplatio*)

Read the Scripture again, followed by this reflection:

≈ What conversion of mind, heart, and life is the Lord asking of me?

_____

_____

_____

_____

≈ *And you, Bethlehem, land of Judah,/ are by no means least among the rulers of Judah* Who is viewed as least in my community? How can I reach out to serve those who are the least?

≈ *When you have found him, bring me word, that I too may go and do him homage.* How have I shared my love for and faith in God with others? When have I invited someone to come to the Lord?

≈ *Then they opened their treasures and offered him gifts of gold, frankincense, and myrrh.* What gifts do I have to offer God? How can I grow in gratitude for the gifts that God has given me?

Closing Prayer

O God, with your judgment endow the king,
    and with your justice, the king's son;
He shall govern your people with justice
    and your afflicted ones with judgment.

Justice shall flower in his days,
    and profound peace, till the moon be no more.
May he rule from sea to sea, and from the River to the ends of the
earth.

The kings of Tarshish and the Isles shall offer gifts;
    the kings of Arabia and Seba shall bring tribute.
All kings shall pay him homage,
    all nations shall serve him.

For he shall rescue the poor when he cries out,
    and the afflicted when he has no one to help him.
He shall have pity for the lowly and the poor;
    the lives of the poor he shall save.

From Psalm 72

Living the Word This Week

How can I make my life a gift for others in charity?

Spend time in prayer before the Blessed Sacrament, offering homage
to the Lord in the Eucharist.

January 15, 2023

Lectio Divina for the Second Week in Ordinary Time

We begin our prayer:

In the name of the Father, and of the Son, and of the Holy Spirit. Amen.

Almighty ever-living God,
who govern all things,
both in heaven and on earth,
mercifully hear the pleading of your people
and bestow your peace on our times.
Through our Lord Jesus Christ, your Son,
who lives and reigns with you in the unity of the Holy Spirit,
God, for ever and ever.

Collect, Second Sunday in Ordinary Time

Reading (*Lectio*)

Read the following Scripture two or three times.

John 1:29-34

> John the Baptist saw Jesus coming toward him and said, "Behold, the Lamb of God, who takes away the sin of the world. He is the one of whom I said, 'A man is coming after me who ranks ahead of me because he existed before me.' I did not know him, but the reason why I came baptizing with water was that he might be made known to Israel." John testified further, saying, "I saw the Spirit come down like a dove from heaven and remain upon him. I did not know him, but the one who sent me to baptize with water told me, 'On whomever you see the Spirit come down and remain, he is the one who will baptize with the Holy Spirit.' Now I have seen and testified that he is the Son of God."

Meditation (*Meditatio*)

After the reading, take some time to reflect in silence on one or more of the following questions:

- What word or words in this passage caught your attention?
- What in this passage comforted you?
- What in this passage challenged you?

If practicing lectio divina *as a family or in a group, after the reflection time, invite the participants to share their responses.*

Prayer (*Oratio*)

Read the scripture passage one more time. Bring to the Lord the praise, petition, or thanksgiving that the Word inspires in you.

Contemplation (*Contemplatio*)

Read the Scripture again, followed by this reflection:

~ What conversion of mind, heart, and life is the Lord asking of me?

_____

_____

_____

_____

~ *John the Baptist saw Jesus coming toward him.* When have I encountered Christ? How can I become more aware of God's presence in those I meet, especially those in need?

_____

_____

_____

_____

~ *I did not know him.* When have I felt far from God? How can I grow in my knowledge of and love for God?

_____

_____

_____

_____

~ *Now I have seen and testified that he is the Son of God.* When have I testified to God's actions in my life? How can I become more comfortable sharing my faith?

_____

_____

_____

_____

~ *After a period of silent reflection and/or discussion, all recite the Lord's Prayer and the following:*

Closing Prayer

I have waited, waited for the LORD,
    and he stooped toward me and heard my cry.
And he put a new song into my mouth,
    a hymn to our God.

Sacrifice or offering you wished not,
    but ears open to obedience you gave me.
Holocausts or sin-offerings you sought not;
    then said I, "Behold I come."

"In the written scroll it is prescribed for me,
to do your will, O my God, is my delight,
    and your law is within my heart!"

I announced your justice in the vast assembly;
    I did not restrain my lips, as you, O LORD, know.

From Psalm 40

Living the Word This Week

How can I make my life a gift for others in charity?

Read *Disciples Called to Witness* to learn how to share your faith more effectively: https://www.usccb.org/beliefs-and-teachings/how-we-teach/new-evangelization/disciples-called-to-witness

January 22, 2023

Lectio Divina for the Third Week in Ordinary Time

We begin our prayer:

In the name of the Father, and of the Son, and of the Holy Spirit. Amen.

Almighty ever-living God,
direct our actions according to your good pleasure,
that in the name of your beloved Son
we may abound in good works.
Through our Lord Jesus Christ, your Son,
who lives and reigns with you in the unity of the Holy Spirit,
God, for ever and ever.

Collect, Third Sunday in Ordinary Time

Reading (*Lectio*)

Read the following Scripture two or three times.

Matthew 4:12-23

When Jesus heard that John had been arrested, he withdrew to Galilee. He left Nazareth and went to live in Capernaum by the sea, in the region of Zebulun and Naphtali, that what had been said through Isaiah the prophet might be fulfilled:

Land of Zebulun and land of Naphtali,
the way to the sea, beyond the Jordan,
Galilee of the Gentiles,
the people who sit in darkness have seen a great light,
on those dwelling in a land overshadowed by death
light has arisen.

From that time on, Jesus began to preach and say, "Repent, for the kingdom of heaven is at hand."

As he was walking by the Sea of Galilee, he saw two brothers, Simon who is called Peter, and his brother Andrew, casting a net into the sea; they were fishermen. He said to them, "Come after me, and I will make you fishers of men." At once they left their nets and followed him. He walked along from there and saw two other brothers, James, the son of Zebedee, and his brother John. They were in a boat, with their father Zebedee, mending their nets. He called them, and immediately they left their boat and their father and followed him. He went around all of Galilee, teaching in their synagogues, proclaiming the gospel of the kingdom, and curing every disease and illness among the people.

Meditation (*Meditatio*)

After the reading, take some time to reflect in silence on one or more of the following questions:

- What word or words in this passage caught your attention?
- What in this passage comforted you?
- What in this passage challenged you?

If practicing lectio divina *as a family or in a group, after the reflection time, invite the participants to share their responses.*

Prayer (*Oratio*)

Read the scripture passage one more time. Bring to the Lord the praise, petition, or thanksgiving that the Word inspires in you.

Contemplation (*Contemplatio*)

Read the Scripture again, followed by this reflection:

≈ What conversion of mind, heart, and life is the Lord asking of me?

_____

_____

_____

_____

≈ *On those dwelling in a land overshadowed by death/ light has arisen.*
How can I maintain a sense of hope in a world where despair is more
common? How can I share that hope with others?

_____

_____

_____

_____

≈ *"Repent, for the kingdom of heaven is at hand."* What sinful behaviors
keep me from following God and obeying his will? What near
occasions of sin do I need to avoid?

_____

_____

_____

_____

≈ *At once they left their nets and followed him.* What distracts me from
following the Lord? How can I become more docile to God's will for me?

_____

_____

_____

_____

≈ After a period of silent reflection and/or discussion, all recite the Lord's Prayer and the following:

Closing Prayer

The LORD is my light and my salvation;
  whom should I fear?
The LORD is my life's refuge;
  of whom should I be afraid?

One thing I ask of the LORD;
  this I seek:
To dwell in the house of the LORD
  all the days of my life,
That I may gaze on the loveliness of the LORD
  and contemplate his temple.

I believe that I shall see the bounty of the LORD
  in the land of the living.
Wait for the LORD with courage;
  be stouthearted, and wait for the LORD.

From Psalm 27

Living the Word This Week

How can I make my life a gift for others in charity?

Pray for those discerning a vocation to the priesthood, consecrated life, or permanent diaconate.

January 29, 2023

Lectio Divina for the Fourth Week in Ordinary Time

We begin our prayer:

In the name of the Father, and of the Son, and of the Holy Spirit. Amen.

Grant us, Lord our God,
that we may honor you with all our mind,
and love everyone in truth of heart.
Through our Lord Jesus Christ, your Son,
who lives and reigns with you in the unity of the Holy Spirit,
God, for ever and ever.

Collect, Fourth Sunday in Ordinary Time

Reading (*Lectio*)

Read the following Scripture two or three times.

Matthew 5:1-12a

When Jesus saw the crowds, he went up the mountain, and after he had sat down, his disciples came to him. He began to teach them, saying:

"Blessed are the poor in spirit,
for theirs is the kingdom of heaven.
Blessed are they who mourn,
for they will be comforted.
Blessed are the meek,
for they will inherit the land.
Blessed are they who hunger and thirst for righteousness,
for they will be satisfied.
Blessed are the merciful,
for they will be shown mercy.
Blessed are the clean of heart,
for they will see God.
Blessed are the peacemakers,
for they will be called children of God.
Blessed are they who are persecuted for the sake of righteousness,
for theirs is the kingdom of heaven.
Blessed are you when they insult you and persecute you
and utter every kind of evil against you falsely because of me.

Rejoice and be glad, for your reward will be great in heaven."

Meditation (*Meditatio*)

After the reading, take some time to reflect in silence on one or more of the following questions:

- What word or words in this passage caught your attention?
- What in this passage comforted you?
- What in this passage challenged you?

If practicing lectio divina *as a family or in a group, after the reflection time, invite the participants to share their responses.*

Prayer (*Oratio*)

Read the scripture passage one more time. Bring to the Lord the praise, petition, or thanksgiving that the Word inspires in you.

Contemplation (*Contemplatio*)

Read the Scripture again, followed by this reflection:

≈ What conversion of mind, heart, and life is the Lord asking of me?

_____

_____

_____

_____

∾ *Blessed are the meek,/ for they will inherit the land.* When have I depended too much on my own strength and abilities? When have I built myself up by diminishing others?

_____

_____

_____

_____

∾ *Blessed are they who hunger and thirst for righteousness,/ for they will be satisfied.* What injustices do I see around me? What actions can I take against violence and injustice?

_____

_____

_____

_____

∾ *Blessed are the merciful,/ for they will be shown mercy.* Who do I need to forgive? From whom do I need to see forgiveness?

_____

_____

_____

_____

≈ *After a period of silent reflection and/or discussion, all recite the Lord's Prayer and the following:*

Closing Prayer

The LORD keeps faith forever,
>secures justice for the oppressed,
>>gives food to the hungry.
The LORD sets captives free.

The LORD gives sight to the blind;
>the LORD raises up those who were bowed down.
The LORD loves the just;
>the LORD protects strangers.

The fatherless and the widow the LORD sustains,
>but the way of the wicked he thwarts.
The LORD shall reign forever;
>your God, O Zion, through all generations. Alleluia.

From Psalm 146

Living the Word This Week

How can I make my life a gift for others in charity?

Join the issue advocacy network of your diocese or state Catholic conference.

February 5, 2023

Lectio Divina for the Fifth Week in Ordinary Time

We begin our prayer:

In the name of the Father, and of the Son, and of the Holy Spirit. Amen.

Keep your family safe, O Lord, with unfailing care,
that, relying solely on the hope of heavenly grace,
they may be defended always by your protection.
Through our Lord Jesus Christ, your Son,
who lives and reigns with you in the unity of the Holy Spirit,
God, for ever and ever.

Collect, Fifth Sunday in Ordinary Time

Reading (*Lectio*)

Read the following Scripture two or three times.

Matthew 5:13-16

> Jesus said to his disciples: "You are the salt of the earth. But if salt loses its taste, with what can it be seasoned? It is no longer good for anything but to be thrown out and trampled underfoot. You are the light of the world. A city set on a mountain cannot be hidden. Nor do they light a lamp and then put it under a bushel basket; it is set on a lampstand, where it gives light to all in the house. Just so, your light must shine before others, that they may see your good deeds and glorify your heavenly Father."

Meditation (*Meditatio*)

After the reading, take some time to reflect in silence on one or more of the following questions:

- What word or words in this passage caught your attention?
- What in this passage comforted you?
- What in this passage challenged you?

If practicing lectio divina *as a family or in a group, after the reflection time, invite the participants to share their responses.*

Prayer (*Oratio*)

Read the scripture passage one more time. Bring to the Lord the praise, petition, or thanksgiving that the Word inspires in you.

Contemplation (*Contemplatio*)

Read the Scripture again, followed by this reflection:

≈ What conversion of mind, heart, and life is the Lord asking of me?

_____

_____

_____

_____

≈ *But if salt loses its taste, with what can it be seasoned?* When have I experienced a dryness in my faith life? How can I take time away to restore and renew my faith?

_____

_____

_____

_____

≈ *A city set on a mountain cannot be hidden.* When have I tried to hide my beliefs to avoid criticism or mocking? How do I demonstrate my faith through my actions?

_____

_____

_____

_____

≈ *Your light must shine before others, that they may see your good deeds and glorify your heavenly Father.* How do my actions point toward God instead of myself? How do I place my God-given gifts in service to my brothers and sisters?

_____

_____

_____

_____

≈ *After a period of silent reflection and/or discussion, all recite the Lord's Prayer and the following:*

Closing Prayer

Light shines through the darkness for the upright;
>   he is gracious and merciful and just.
Well for the man who is gracious and lends,
>   who conducts his affairs with justice.

He shall never be moved;
>   the just one shall be in everlasting remembrance.
An evil report he shall not fear;
>   his heart is firm, trusting in the LORD.

His heart is steadfast; he shall not fear.
  Lavishly he gives to the poor;
His justice shall endure forever;
  his horn shall be exalted in glory.

From Psalm 112

Living the Word This Week

How can I make my life a gift for others in charity?

Pray for those who lack the freedom to live their faith in its fullness.

February 12, 2023

Lectio Divina for the Sixth Week in Ordinary Time

We begin our prayer:

In the name of the Father, and of the Son, and of the Holy Spirit. Amen.

O God, who teach us that you abide
in hearts that are just and true,
grant that we may be so fashioned by your grace
as to become a dwelling pleasing to you.
Through our Lord Jesus Christ, your Son,
who lives and reigns with you in the unity of the Holy Spirit,
God, for ever and ever.

Collect, Sixth Sunday in Ordinary Time

Reading (*Lectio*)

Read the following Scripture two or three times.

Matthew 5:20-22a, 27-28, 33-34a, 37

> Jesus said to his disciples: "I tell you, unless your righteousness surpasses that of the scribes and Pharisees, you will not enter the kingdom of heaven.
>
> "You have heard that it was said to your ancestors, *You shall not kill; and whoever kills will be liable to judgment.* But I say to you, whoever is angry with brother will be liable to judgment.
>
> "You have heard that it was said, *You shall not commit adultery.* But I say to you, everyone who looks at a woman with lust has already committed adultery with her in his heart.
>
> "Again you have heard that it was said to your ancestors, *Do not take a false oath, but make good to the Lord all that you vow.* But I say to you, do not swear at all. Let your 'Yes' mean 'Yes,' and your 'No' mean 'No.' Anything more is from the evil one."

Meditation (*Meditatio*)

After the reading, take some time to reflect in silence on one or more of the following questions:

- What word or words in this passage caught your attention?
- What in this passage comforted you?
- What in this passage challenged you?

If practicing lectio divina *as a family or in a group, after the reflection time, invite the participants to share their responses.*

Prayer (*Oratio*)

Read the scripture passage one more time. Bring to the Lord the praise, petition, or thanksgiving that the Word inspires in you.

Contemplation (*Contemplatio*)

Read the Scripture again, followed by this reflection:

∼ What conversion of mind, heart, and life is the Lord asking of me?

_____

_____

_____

_____

∼ *"You have heard that it was said to your ancestors...."* How have my relatives and friends taught me about the faith? How can I learn from the examples of the holy ones who have gone before me?

_____

_____

_____

_____

~ *"Whoever is angry with brother will be liable to judgment."* How do I treat those closest to me? How can I grow in patience and in love for my brothers and sisters?

_____

_____

_____

_____

~ *"Let your 'Yes' mean 'Yes,' and your 'No' mean 'No.'"* Am I a person of my word? Do my actions back up what I profess to believe?

_____

_____

_____

_____

~ *After a period of silent reflection and/or discussion, all recite the Lord's Prayer and the following:*

Closing Prayer

Blessed are they whose way is blameless,
  who walk in the law of the LORD.
Blessed are they who observe his decrees,
  who seek him with all their heart.

You have commanded that your precepts
     be diligently kept.
Oh, that I might be firm in the ways
     of keeping your statutes!

Be good to your servant, that I may live
     and keep your words.
Open my eyes, that I may consider
     the wonders of your law.

Instruct me, O Lord, in the way of your statutes,
     that I may exactly observe them.
Give me discernment, that I may observe your law
     and keep it with all my heart.

From Psalm 119

Living the Word This Week

How can I make my life a gift for others in charity?

Research volunteer opportunities in your parish, diocese, or community and put your talents to work for the common good.

February 19, 2023

Lectio Divina for the Seventh Week in Ordinary Time

We begin our prayer:

In the name of the Father, and of the Son, and of the Holy Spirit. Amen.

Grant, we pray, almighty God,
that, always pondering spiritual things,
we may carry out in both word and deed
that which is pleasing to you.
Through our Lord Jesus Christ, your Son,
who lives and reigns with you in the unity of the Holy Spirit,
God, for ever and ever.

Collect, Seventh Sunday in Ordinary Time

Reading (*Lectio*)

Read the following Scripture two or three times.

Matthew 5:38-48

> Jesus said to his disciples: "You have heard that it was said, *An eye for an eye and a tooth for a tooth.* But I say to you, offer no resistance to one who is evil. When someone strikes you on your right cheek, turn the other one as well. If anyone wants to go to law with you over your tunic, hand over your cloak as well. Should anyone press you into service for one mile, go for two miles. Give to the one who asks of you, and do not turn your back on one who wants to borrow.
>
> "You have heard that it was said, *You shall love your neighbor and hate your enemy.* But I say to you, love your enemies and pray for those who persecute you, that you may be children of your heavenly Father, for he makes his sun rise on the bad and the good, and causes rain to fall on the just and the unjust. For if you love those who love you, what recompense will you have? Do not the tax collectors do the same? And if you greet your brothers only, what is unusual about that? Do not the pagans do the same? So be perfect, just as your heavenly Father is perfect."

Meditation (*Meditatio*)

After the reading, take some time to reflect in silence on one or more of the following questions:

- What word or words in this passage caught your attention?
- What in this passage comforted you?
- What in this passage challenged you?

If practicing lectio divina *as a family or in a group, after the reflection time, invite the participants to share their responses.*

Prayer (*Oratio*)

Read the scripture passage one more time. Bring to the Lord the praise, petition, or thanksgiving that the Word inspires in you.

Contemplation (*Contemplatio*)

Read the Scripture again, followed by this reflection:

≈ What conversion of mind, heart, and life is the Lord asking of me?

_____

_____

_____

_____

≈ *Should anyone press you into service for one mile, go for two miles.* How can I be of service to those in need? How can I share my time with greater generosity?

_____

_____

_____

_____

≈ *Give to the one who asks of you, and do not turn your back on one who wants to borrow.* How do I view those who are poor and lack worldly goods? How do I support structures that keep people in poverty?

_____

_____

_____

_____

≈ *For if you love those who love you, what recompense will you have?* Who needs my love and kindness? What keeps me from loving them?

_____

_____

_____

_____

≈ *After a period of silent reflection and/or discussion, all recite the Lord's Prayer and the following:*

Closing Prayer

Bless the LORD, O my soul;
    and all my being, bless his holy name.
Bless the LORD, O my soul,
    and forget not all his benefits.

He pardons all your iniquities,
 heals all your ills.
He redeems your life from destruction,
 crowns you with kindness and compassion.

Merciful and gracious is the LORD,
 slow to anger and abounding in kindness.
Not according to our sins does he deal with us,
 nor does he requite us according to our crimes.

As far as the east is from the west,
 so far has he put our transgressions from us.
As a father has compassion on his children,
 so the LORD has compassion on those who fear him.

From Psalm 103

Living the Word This Week

How can I make my life a gift for others in charity?

Learn more about becoming a Christian steward: https://www.usccb.org/committees/evangelization-catechesis/stewardship

February 22, 2023

Lectio Divina for Ash Wednesday

We begin our prayer:

In the name of the Father, and of the Son, and of the Holy Spirit. Amen.

Almighty ever-living God,
look with compassion on our weakness
and ensure us your protection
by stretching forth the right hand of your majesty.
Through our Lord Jesus Christ, your Son,
who lives and reigns with you in the unity of the Holy Spirit,
God, for ever and ever.

Collect, Saturday after Ash Wednesday

Reading (*Lectio*)

Read the following Scripture two or three times.

Matthew 6:1-6, 16-18

> Jesus said to his disciples: "Take care not to perform righteous
> deeds in order that people may see them; otherwise, you will have

no recompense from your heavenly Father. When you give alms, do not blow a trumpet before you, as the hypocrites do in the synagogues and in the streets to win the praise of others. Amen, I say to you, they have received their reward. But when you give alms, do not let your left hand know what your right is doing, so that your almsgiving may be secret. And your Father who sees in secret will repay you.

"When you pray, do not be like the hypocrites, who love to stand and pray in the synagogues and on street corners so that others may see them. Amen, I say to you, they have received their reward. But when you pray, go to your inner room, close the door, and pray to your Father in secret. And your Father who sees in secret will repay you.

"When you fast, do not look gloomy like the hypocrites. They neglect their appearance, so that they may appear to others to be fasting. Amen, I say to you, they have received their reward. But when you fast, anoint your head and wash your face, so that you may not appear to be fasting, except to your Father who is hidden. And your Father who sees what is hidden will repay you."

Meditation (*Meditatio*)

After the reading, take some time to reflect in silence on one or more of the following questions:

- What word or words in this passage caught your attention?
- What in this passage comforted you?
- What in this passage challenged you?

If practicing lectio divina *as a family or in a group, after the reflection time, invite the participants to share their responses.*

Prayer (*Oratio*)

Read the scripture passage one more time. Bring to the Lord the praise, petition, or thanksgiving that the Word inspires in you.

Contemplation (*Contemplatio*)

Read the Scripture again, followed by this reflection:

≈ What conversion of mind, heart, and life is the Lord asking of me?

_____

_____

_____

_____

≈ *Take care not to perform righteous deeds in order that people may see them.* What motivates me to perform righteous deeds? How can I purify my motivation?

_____

_____

_____

_____

≈ *When you pray, go to your inner room, close the door, and pray to your Father in secret.* Where can I pray without distraction? What time in my day is dedicated to prayer?

_____

_____

_____

_____

≈ *And your Father who sees what is hidden will repay you.* What parts of me does only God know? How do I experience God's loving kindness and favor?

_____

_____

_____

_____

≈ *After a period of silent reflection and/or discussion, all recite the Lord's Prayer and the following:*

Closing Prayer

Have mercy on me, O God, in your goodness;
    in the greatness of your compassion wipe out my offense.
Thoroughly wash me from my guilt
    and of my sin cleanse me.

For I acknowledge my offense,
　　and my sin is before me always:
"Against you only have I sinned,
　　and done what is evil in your sight."

A clean heart create for me, O God,
　　and a steadfast spirit renew within me.
Cast me not out from your presence,
　　and your Holy Spirit take not from me.

Give me back the joy of your salvation,
　　and a willing spirit sustain in me.
O Lord, open my lips,
　　and my mouth shall proclaim your praise.

From Psalm 51

Living the Word This Week

How can I make my life a gift for others in charity?

Decide how you will observe Lent with practices of prayer, fasting, and almsgiving.

February 26, 2023

Lectio Divina for the First Week of Lent

We begin our prayer:

In the name of the Father, and of the Son, and of the Holy Spirit. Amen.

Bestow on us, we pray, O Lord,
a spirit of always pondering on what is right
and of hastening to carry it out,
and, since without you we cannot exist,
may we be enabled to live according to your will.
Through our Lord Jesus Christ, your Son,
who lives and reigns with you in the unity of the Holy Spirit,
God, for ever and ever.

Collect, Thursday of the First Week of Lent

Reading (*Lectio*)

Read the following Scripture two or three times.

Matthew 4:1-11

At that time Jesus was led by the Spirit into the desert to be
tempted by the devil. He fasted for forty days and forty nights,

and afterwards he was hungry. The tempter approached and said to him, "If you are the Son of God, command that these stones become loaves of bread."

He said in reply, "It is written:

One does not live on bread alone,
  but on every word that comes forth
  from the mouth of God."

Then the devil took him to the holy city, and made him stand on the parapet of the temple, and said to him, "If you are the Son of God, throw yourself down. For it is written:

He will command his angels concerning you
  and with their hands they will support you,
lest you dash your foot against a stone."

Jesus answered him, "Again it is written,

You shall not put the Lord, your God, to the test."

Then the devil took him up to a very high mountain, and showed him all the kingdoms of the world in their magnificence, and he said to him, "All these I shall give to you, if you will prostrate yourself and worship me." At this, Jesus said to him, "Get away, Satan! It is written:

The Lord, your God, shall you worship
  and him alone shall you serve."

Then the devil left him and, behold, angels came and ministered to him.

Meditation (*Meditatio*)

After the reading, take some time to reflect in silence on one or more of the following questions:

- What word or words in this passage caught your attention?
- What in this passage comforted you?
- What in this passage challenged you?

If practicing lectio divina *as a family or in a group, after the reflection time, invite the participants to share their responses.*

Prayer (*Oratio*)

Read the scripture passage one more time. Bring to the Lord the praise, petition, or thanksgiving that the Word inspires in you.

Contemplation (*Contemplatio*)

Read the Scripture again, followed by this reflection:

∾ What conversion of mind, heart, and life is the Lord asking of me?

_____

_____

_____

_____

≈ *At that time Jesus was led by the Spirit into the desert to be tempted by the devil.* What temptations lead me away from God? How can I be led by the Spirit instead?

_____

_____

_____

_____

≈ *You shall not put the Lord, your God, to the test.* When have I tried to test God's love for me? How can I grow in my trust for God's Divine Providence?

_____

_____

_____

_____

≈ *All these I shall give to you, if you will prostrate yourself and worship me.* Do I own my possessions or do my possessions own me? How does my pursuit of worldly comfort distract me from God and from the needs of my brothers and sisters?

_____

_____

_____

_____

~ *After a period of silent reflection and/or discussion, all recite the Lord's Prayer and the following:*

Closing Prayer

Have mercy on me, O God, in your goodness;
    in the greatness of your compassion wipe out my offense.
Thoroughly wash me from my guilt
    and of my sin cleanse me.

For I acknowledge my offense,
    and my sin is before me always:
"Against you only have I sinned,
    and done what is evil in your sight."

A clean heart create for me, O God,
    and a steadfast spirit renew within me.
Cast me not out from your presence,
    and your Holy Spirit take not from me.

Give me back the joy of your salvation,
    and a willing spirit sustain in me.
O Lord, open my lips,
    and my mouth shall proclaim your praise.

From Psalm 51

Living the Word This Week

How can I make my life a gift for others in charity?

Make a good examination of conscience and plan to receive the Sacrament of Penance during Lent.

March 5, 2023

Lectio Divina for the Second Week of Lent

We begin our prayer:

In the name of the Father, and of the Son, and of the Holy Spirit. Amen.

Guard your Church, we pray, O Lord, in your unceasing mercy,
and, since without you mortal humanity is sure to fall,
may we be kept by your constant helps from all harm
and directed to all that brings salvation.
Through our Lord Jesus Christ, your Son,
who lives and reigns with you in the unity of the Holy Spirit,
God, for ever and ever.

Collect, Tuesday of the Second Week of Lent

Reading (*Lectio*)

Read the following Scripture two or three times.

Matthew 17:1-9

> Jesus took Peter, James, and John his brother, and led them up
> a high mountain by themselves. And he was transfigured before

them; his face shone like the sun and his clothes became white as light. And behold, Moses and Elijah appeared to them, conversing with him. Then Peter said to Jesus in reply, "Lord, it is good that we are here. If you wish, I will make three tents here, one for you, one for Moses, and one for Elijah." While he was still speaking, behold, a bright cloud cast a shadow over them, then from the cloud came a voice that said, "This is my beloved Son, with whom I am well pleased; listen to him." When the disciples heard this, they fell prostrate and were very much afraid. But Jesus came and touched them, saying, "Rise, and do not be afraid." And when the disciples raised their eyes, they saw no one else but Jesus alone.

As they were coming down from the mountain, Jesus charged them, "Do not tell the vision to anyone until the Son of Man has been raised from the dead."

Meditation (*Meditatio*)

After the reading, take some time to reflect in silence on one or more of the following questions:

- What word or words in this passage caught your attention?
- What in this passage comforted you?
- What in this passage challenged you?

If practicing lectio divina *as a family or in a group, after the reflection time, invite the participants to share their responses.*

Prayer (*Oratio*)

Read the scripture passage one more time. Bring to the Lord the praise, petition, or thanksgiving that the Word inspires in you.

Contemplation (*Contemplatio*)

Read the Scripture again, followed by this reflection:

∿ What conversion of mind, heart, and life is the Lord asking of me?

_____

_____

_____

_____

∿ *And he was transfigured before them; his face shone like the sun and his clothes became white as light.* How has God's grace transformed my life? How can my faith shine in my life?

_____

_____

_____

_____

∿ *"This is my beloved Son, with whom I am well pleased; listen to him."* How do I hear the voice of the Lord? How can I listen to him more attentively?

_____

_____

～ *They saw no one else but Jesus alone.* How can I keep my gaze fixed on Jesus? How can I focus on Jesus alone?

_____

_____

_____

_____

～ *After a period of silent reflection and/or discussion, all recite the Lord's Prayer and the following:*

Closing Prayer

Upright is the word of the LORD,
  and all his works are trustworthy.
He loves justice and right;
  of the kindness of the LORD the earth is full.

See, the eyes of the LORD are upon those who fear him,
  upon those who hope for his kindness,
To deliver them from death
  and preserve them in spite of famine.

Our soul waits for the Lord,
    who is our help and our shield.
May your kindness, O Lord, be upon us
    who have put our hope in you.

From Psalm 33

Living the Word This Week

How can I make my life a gift for others in charity?

Attend daily Mass at least one day this week and be very attentive to the prayers and gestures of the Mass.

March 12, 2023

Lectio Divina for the Third Week of Lent

We begin our prayer:

In the name of the Father, and of the Son, and of the Holy Spirit. Amen.

Grant, we pray, O Lord,
that, schooled through Lenten observance
and nourished by your word,
through holy restraint
we may be devoted to you with all our heart
and be ever united in prayer.
Through our Lord Jesus Christ, your Son,
who lives and reigns with you in the unity of the Holy Spirit,
God, for ever and ever.

Collect, Wednesday of the Third Week of Lent

Reading (*Lectio*)

Read the following Scripture two or three times.

John 4:5-15, 19b-26, 39a, 40-42

Jesus came to a town of Samaria called Sychar, near the plot of land that Jacob had given to his son Joseph. Jacob's well was there. Jesus, tired from his journey, sat down there at the well. It was about noon.

A woman of Samaria came to draw water. Jesus said to her, "Give me a drink." His disciples had gone into the town to buy food. The Samaritan woman said to him, "How can you, a Jew, ask me, a Samaritan woman, for a drink?" —For Jews use nothing in common with Samaritans.— Jesus answered and said to her, "If you knew the gift of God and who is saying to you, 'Give me a drink,' you would have asked him and he would have given you living water." The woman said to him, "Sir, you do not even have a bucket and the cistern is deep; where then can you get this living water? Are you greater than our father Jacob, who gave us this cistern and drank from it himself with his children and his flocks?" Jesus answered and said to her, "Everyone who drinks this water will be thirsty again; but whoever drinks the water I shall give will never thirst; the water I shall give will become in him a spring of water welling up to eternal life." The woman said to him, "Sir, give me this water, so that I may not be thirsty or have to keep coming here to draw water.

"I can see that you are a prophet. Our ancestors worshiped on this mountain; but you people say that the place to worship is in Jerusalem." Jesus said to her, "Believe me, woman, the hour is coming when you will worship the Father neither on this mountain nor in Jerusalem. You people worship what you do not understand; we worship what we understand, because salvation is from the Jews. But the hour is coming, and is now here, when true worshipers will worship the Father in Spirit and truth; and indeed the Father seeks such people to worship him. God is Spirit, and those who worship him must worship in Spirit and truth." The woman said to him, "I know that the Messiah is coming, the one called the Christ; when he comes, he will tell us everything." Jesus said to her, "I am he, the one who is speaking with you."

Many of the Samaritans of that town began to believe in him. When the Samaritans came to him, they invited him to stay with them; and he stayed there two days. Many more began to believe in him because of his word, and they said to the woman, "We no longer believe because of your word; for we have heard for ourselves, and we know that this is truly the savior of the world."

Meditation (*Meditatio*)

After the reading, take some time to reflect in silence on one or more of the following questions:

- What word or words in this passage caught your attention?
- What in this passage comforted you?
- What in this passage challenged you?

If practicing lectio divina *as a family or in a group, after the reflection time, invite the participants to share their responses.*

Prayer (*Oratio*)

Read the scripture passage one more time. Bring to the Lord the praise, petition, or thanksgiving that the Word inspires in you.

Contemplation (*Contemplatio*)

Read the Scripture again, followed by this reflection:

∾ What conversion of mind, heart, and life is the Lord asking of me?

_____

_____

_____

_____

∾ *The Samaritan woman said to him, "How can you, a Jew, ask me, a Samaritan woman, for a drink?"* Who do I exclude from the circle of my concern? To whom should I reach out in love and service?

_____

_____

_____

_____

∾ *I can see that you are a prophet.* Who in my life speaks uncomfortable truths? What prophetic voices should I listen for?

_____

_____

_____

_____

~ *We worship what we understand.* How well do I understand my faith? How can I grow in knowledge and understanding?

_____

_____

_____

_____

~ *After a period of silent reflection and/or discussion, all recite the Lord's Prayer and the following:*

Closing Prayer

Come, let us sing joyfully to the LORD;
  let us acclaim the Rock of our salvation.
Let us come into his presence with thanksgiving;
  let us joyfully sing psalms to him.

Come, let us bow down in worship;
  let us kneel before the LORD who made us.
For he is our God,
  and we are the people he shepherds, the flock he guides.

Oh, that today you would hear his voice:
> "Harden not your hearts as at Meribah,
> as in the day of Massah in the desert,
Where your fathers tempted me;
> they tested me though they had seen my works."

From Psalm 95

Living the Word This Week

How can I make my life a gift for others in charity?

During the week, make a visit to a church to pray the Stations of the Cross.

March 19, 2021

Lectio Divina for the Fourth Week of Lent

We begin our prayer:

In the name of the Father, and of the Son, and of the Holy Spirit. Amen.

O God, who renew the world
through mysteries beyond all telling,
grant, we pray,
that your Church may be guided by your eternal design
and not be deprived of your help in this present age.
Through our Lord Jesus Christ, your Son,
who lives and reigns with you in the unity of the Holy Spirit,
God, for ever and ever.

Collect, Monday of the Fourth Week of Lent

Reading (*Lectio*)

Read the following Scripture two or three times.

John 9:1, 6-9, 13-17, 34-38

As Jesus passed by he saw a man blind from birth. He spat on the ground and made clay with the saliva, and smeared the clay on his eyes, and said to him, "Go wash in the Pool of Siloam" — which means Sent —. So he went and washed, and came back able to see.

His neighbors and those who had seen him earlier as a beggar said, "Isn't this the one who used to sit and beg?" Some said, "It is," but others said, "No, he just looks like him." He said, "I am."

They brought the one who was once blind to the Pharisees. Now Jesus had made clay and opened his eyes on a sabbath. So then the Pharisees also asked him how he was able to see.

He said to them, "He put clay on my eyes, and I washed, and now I can see." So some of the Pharisees said, "This man is not from God, because he does not keep the sabbath." But others said, "How can a sinful man do such signs?" And there was a division among them. So they said to the blind man again, "What do you have to say about him, since he opened your eyes?" He said, "He is a prophet."

They answered and said to him, "You were born totally in sin, and are you trying to teach us?" Then they threw him out.

When Jesus heard that they had thrown him out, he found him and said, "Do you believe in the Son of Man?" He answered and said, "Who is he, sir, that I may believe in him?" Jesus said to him, "You have seen him, and the one speaking with you is he." He said, "I do believe, Lord," and he worshiped him.

Meditation (*Meditatio*)

After the reading, take some time to reflect in silence on one or more of the following questions:

- What word or words in this passage caught your attention?
- What in this passage comforted you?
- What in this passage challenged you?

If practicing lectio divina *as a family or in a group, after the reflection time, invite the participants to share their responses.*

Prayer (*Oratio*)

Read the scripture passage one more time. Bring to the Lord the praise, petition, or thanksgiving that the Word inspires in you.

Contemplation (*Contemplatio*)

Read the Scripture again, followed by this reflection:

≈ What conversion of mind, heart, and life is the Lord asking of me?

_____

_____

_____

_____

≈ *"Go wash in the Pool of Siloam" — which means Sent —.* Where is God sending me? How am I responding to God's call?

_____

_____

_____

_____

≈ *They brought the one who was once blind to the Pharisees.* How have I failed to see my own sinfulness and God's grace? How can I open my eyes and heart to God's love and mercy active in my life?

_____

_____

_____

_____

≈ *Who is he, sir, that I may believe in him?* How would I describe Jesus to someone who does not know him? How can I come to know Jesus better?

_____

_____

_____

_____

≈ After a period of silent reflection and/or discussion, all recite the
Lord's Prayer and the following:

Closing Prayer

The LORD is my shepherd; I shall not want.
    In verdant pastures he gives me repose;
beside restful waters he leads me;
    he refreshes my soul.

He guides me in right paths
    for his name's sake.
Even though I walk in the dark valley
    I fear no evil; for you are at my side
With your rod and your staff
    that give me courage.

You spread the table before me
    in the sight of my foes;
you anoint my head with oil;
    my cup overflows.

Only goodness and kindness follow me
    all the days of my life;
and I shall dwell in the house of the LORD
    for years to come.

From Psalm 23

Living the Word This Week

How can I make my life a gift for others in charity?

Read Chapter Seven of the *United States Catholic Catechism for Adults* to grow in your knowledge of Jesus Christ: https://www.usccb.org/sites/default/files/flipbooks/uscca/files/assets/basic-html/page-105.html

March 26, 2023

Lectio Divina for the Fifth Week of Lent

We begin our prayer:

In the name of the Father, and of the Son, and of the Holy Spirit. Amen.

Be near, O Lord, to those who plead before you,
and look kindly on those who place their hope in your mercy,
that, cleansed from the stain of their sins,
they may persevere in holy living
and be made full heirs of your promise.
Through our Lord Jesus Christ, your Son,
who lives and reigns with you in the unity of the Holy Spirit,
God, for ever and ever.

Collect, Thursday of the Fifth Week of Lent

Reading (*Lectio*)

Read the following Scripture two or three times.

John 11:3-7, 17, 20-27, 33b-45

The sisters of Lazarus sent word to Jesus, saying, "Master, the one you love is ill." When Jesus heard this he said, "This illness is not to end in death, but is for the glory of God, that the Son of God may be glorified through it." Now Jesus loved Martha and her sister and Lazarus. So when he heard that he was ill, he remained for two days in the place where he was. Then after this he said to his disciples, "Let us go back to Judea."

When Jesus arrived, he found that Lazarus had already been in the tomb for four days. When Martha heard that Jesus was coming, she went to meet him; but Mary sat at home. Martha said to Jesus, "Lord, if you had been here, my brother would not have died. But even now I know that whatever you ask of God, God will give you." Jesus said to her, "Your brother will rise." Martha said, "I know he will rise, in the resurrection on the last day." Jesus told her, "I am the resurrection and the life; whoever believes in me, even if he dies, will live, and everyone who lives and believes in me will never die. Do you believe this?" She said to him, "Yes, Lord. I have come to believe that you are the Christ, the Son of God, the one who is coming into the world."

He became perturbed and deeply troubled, and said, "Where have you laid him?" They said to him, "Sir, come and see." And Jesus wept. So the Jews said, "See how he loved him." But some of them said, "Could not the one who opened the eyes of the blind man have done something so that this man would not have died?"

So Jesus, perturbed again, came to the tomb. It was a cave, and a stone lay across it. Jesus said, "Take away the stone." Martha, the dead man's sister, said to him, "Lord, by now there will be a stench; he has been dead for four days." Jesus said to her, "Did I not tell you that if you believe you will see the glory of God?" So they took away the stone. And Jesus raised his eyes and said, "Father, I thank you for hearing me. I know that you always hear me; but because of the crowd here I have said this, that they may believe that you sent me." And when he had said this, He cried out in a loud voice, "Lazarus, come out!" The dead man came out, tied hand and foot with burial bands, and his face was wrapped in a cloth. So Jesus said to them, "Untie him and let him go."

Now many of the Jews who had come to Mary and seen what he had done began to believe in him.

Meditation (*Meditatio*)

After the reading, take some time to reflect in silence on one or more of the following questions:

- What word or words in this passage caught your attention?
- What in this passage comforted you?
- What in this passage challenged you?

If practicing lectio divina *as a family or in a group, after the reflection time, invite the participants to share their responses.*

Prayer (*Oratio*)

Read the scripture passage one more time. Bring to the Lord the praise, petition, or thanksgiving that the Word inspires in you.

Contemplation (*Contemplatio*)

Read the Scripture again, followed by this reflection:

≈ What conversion of mind, heart, and life is the Lord asking of me?

_____

_____

_____

_____

≈ *This illness is not to end in death, but is for the glory of God, that the Son of God may be glorified through it.* How have I experienced God's glory and felt his presence? How can I glorify God through my life?

_____

_____

_____

_____

≈ *I am the resurrection and the life; whoever believes in me, even if he dies, will live.* What do I imagine that heaven will be like? How do I nurture the hope of eternal life?

_____

_____

_____

_____

≈ *Now many of the Jews who had come to Mary and seen what he had done began to believe in him.* What people and experiences have helped me grow in faith? How can I share my faith with those I meet?

_____

_____

_____

_____

≈ *After a period of silent reflection and/or discussion, all recite the Lord's Prayer and the following:*

Closing Prayer

Out of the depths I cry to you, O LORD;
   LORD, hear my voice!
Let your ears be attentive
   to my voice in supplication.

If you, O LORD, mark iniquities,
   LORD, who can stand?
But with you is forgiveness,
   that you may be revered.

I trust in the Lord;
　　my soul trusts in his word.
More than sentinels wait for the dawn,
　　let Israel wait for the Lord.

For with the Lord is kindness
　　and with him is plenteous redemption;
And he will redeem Israel
　　from all their iniquities.

From Psalm 130

Living the Word This Week

How can I make my life a gift for others in charity?

Invite someone to rediscover their faith: http://www.usccb.org/
beliefs-and-teachings/how-we-teach/new-evangelization/
rediscovering-the-faith/index.cfm

April 2, 2021

Lectio Divina for Holy Week

We begin our prayer:

In the name of the Father, and of the Son, and of the Holy Spirit. Amen.

O God, who willed your Son to submit for our sake
to the yoke of the Cross,
so that you might drive from us the power of the enemy,
grant us, your servants, to attain the grace of the resurrection.
Through our Lord Jesus Christ, your Son,
who lives and reigns with you in the unity of the Holy Spirit,
God, for ever and ever.

Collect, Wednesday of Holy Week

Reading (*Lectio*)

Read the following Scripture two or three times.

Matthew 26: 31-46

> Then Jesus said to them, "This night all of you will have your faith
> in me shaken, for it is written:

> *I will strike the shepherd,*
>   *and the sheep of the flock will be dispersed;*

but after I have been raised up, I shall go before you to Galilee." Peter said to him in reply, "Though all may have their faith in you shaken, mine will never be." Jesus said to him, "Amen, I say to you, this very night before the cock crows, you will deny me three times." Peter said to him, "Even though I should have to die with you, I will not deny you." And all the disciples spoke likewise.

Then Jesus came with them to a place called Gethsemane, and he said to his disciples, "Sit here while I go over there and pray." He took along Peter and the two sons of Zebedee, and began to feel sorrow and distress. Then he said to them, "My soul is sorrowful even to death. Remain here and keep watch with me." He advanced a little and fell prostrate in prayer, saying, "My Father, if it is possible, let this cup pass from me; yet, not as I will, but as you will." When he returned to his disciples he found them asleep. He said to Peter, "So you could not keep watch with me for one hour? Watch and pray that you may not undergo the test. The spirit is willing, but the flesh is weak." Withdrawing a second time, he prayed again, "My Father, if it is not possible that this cup pass without my drinking it, your will be done!" Then he returned once more and found them asleep, for they could not keep their eyes open. He left them and withdrew again and prayed a third time, saying the same thing again. Then he returned to his disciples and said to them, "Are you still sleeping and taking your rest? Behold, the hour is at hand when the Son of Man is to be handed over to sinners. Get up, let us go. Look, my betrayer is at hand."

Meditation (*Meditatio*)

After the reading, take some time to reflect in silence on one or more of the following questions:

- What word or words in this passage caught your attention?
- What in this passage comforted you?
- What in this passage challenged you?

If practicing lectio divina *as a family or in a group, after the reflection time, invite the participants to share their responses.*

Prayer (*Oratio*)

Read the scripture passage one more time. Bring to the Lord the praise, petition, or thanksgiving that the Word inspires in you.

Contemplation (*Contemplatio*)

Read the Scripture again, followed by this reflection:

≈ What conversion of mind, heart, and life is the Lord asking of me?

_____

_____

_____

_____

~ *Though all may have their faith in you shaken, mine will never be.* When has my faith been tested or shaken? How can I seek God's grace to strengthen my faith?

_____

_____

_____

_____

~ *"My Father, if it is possible, let this cup pass from me; yet, not as I will, but as you will."* When has God asked me to do something I found difficult? How can I be more eager to follow God's will for me?

_____

_____

_____

_____

~ *The spirit is willing, but the flesh is weak.* What weaknesses keep me from living an authentic Christian life of love and service? How can I discipline my will so that I follow the Spirit's promptings?

_____

_____

~ *After a period of silent reflection and/or discussion, all recite the Lord's Prayer and the following:*

Closing Prayer

All who see me scoff at me;
    they mock me with parted lips, they wag their heads:
"He relied on the LORD; let him deliver him,
    let him rescue him, if he loves him."

Indeed, many dogs surround me,
    a pack of evildoers closes in upon me;
They have pierced my hands and my feet;
    I can count all my bones.

They divide my garments among them,
    and for my vesture they cast lots.
But you, O LORD, be not far from me;
    O my help, hasten to aid me.

I will proclaim your name to my brethren;
    in the midst of the assembly I will praise you:
"You who fear the LORD, praise him;
    all you descendants of Jacob, give glory to him;
        revere him, all you descendants of Israel!"

From Psalm 22

Living the Word This Week

How can I make my life a gift for others in charity?

Spend time this week meditating on the Lord's Passion and offering your daily struggles and sufferings in union with him.

April 6, 2023

Lectio Divina for the Paschal Triduum

We begin our prayer:

In the name of the Father, and of the Son, and of the Holy Spirit. Amen.

Almighty ever-living God,
who have restored us to life
by the blessed Death and Resurrection of your Christ,
preserve in us the work of your mercy,
that, by partaking of this mystery,
we may have a life unceasingly devoted to you.
Through Christ our Lord.

Prayer after Communion, Good Friday

Reading (*Lectio*)

Read the following Scripture two or three times.

John 13:1-15

> Before the feast of Passover, Jesus knew that his hour had come to
> pass from this world to the Father. He loved his own in the world

and he loved them to the end. The devil had already induced Judas, son of Simon the Iscariot, to hand him over. So, during supper, fully aware that the Father had put everything into his power and that he had come from God and was returning to God, he rose from supper and took off his outer garments. He took a towel and tied it around his waist. Then he poured water into a basin and began to wash the disciples' feet and dry them with the towel around his waist. He came to Simon Peter, who said to him, "Master, are you going to wash my feet?" Jesus answered and said to him, "What I am doing, you do not understand now, but you will understand later." Peter said to him, "You will never wash my feet." Jesus answered him, "Unless I wash you, you will have no inheritance with me." Simon Peter said to him, "Master, then not only my feet, but my hands and head as well." Jesus said to him, "Whoever has bathed has no need except to have his feet washed, for he is clean all over; so you are clean, but not all." For he knew who would betray him; for this reason, he said, "Not all of you are clean."

So when he had washed their feet and put his garments back on and reclined at table again, he said to them, "Do you realize what I have done for you? You call me 'teacher' and 'master,' and rightly so, for indeed I am. If I, therefore, the master and teacher, have washed your feet, you ought to wash one another's feet. I have given you a model to follow, so that as I have done for you, you should also do."

Meditation (*Meditatio*)

After the reading, take some time to reflect in silence on one or more of the following questions:

- What word or words in this passage caught your attention?
- What in this passage comforted you?
- What in this passage challenged you?

If practicing lectio divina *as a family or in a group, after the reflection time, invite the participants to share their responses.*

Prayer (*Oratio*)

Read the scripture passage one more time. Bring to the Lord the praise, petition, or thanksgiving that the Word inspires in you.

Contemplation (*Contemplatio*)

Read the Scripture again, followed by this reflection:

～ What conversion of mind, heart, and life is the Lord asking of me?

_____

_____

_____

_____

≈ *He had come from God and was returning to God.* Where have I come from? Where am I going?

_____

_____

_____

_____

≈ *What I am doing, you do not understand now, but you will understand later.* What parts of my faith do I struggle to understand? How can I grow in my understanding of God and his Church?

_____

_____

_____

_____

≈ *I have given you a model to follow, so that as I have done for you, you should also do.* What acts of service is God calling me to? How do I share my faith in Jesus through my actions?

_____

_____

_____

_____

∿ *After a period of silent reflection and/or discussion, all recite the Lord's Prayer and the following:*

Closing Prayer

How shall I make a return to the LORD
    for all the good he has done for me?
The cup of salvation I will take up,
    and I will call upon the name of the LORD.

Precious in the eyes of the LORD
    is the death of his faithful ones.
I am your servant, the son of your handmaid;
    you have loosed my bonds.

To you will I offer sacrifice of thanksgiving,
    and I will call upon the name of the LORD.
My vows to the LORD I will pay
    in the presence of all his people.

From Psalm 116

Living the Word This Week

How can I make my life a gift for others in charity?

Prayerfully consider ways that you can serve your brothers and sisters, especially the poor and marginalized.

April 9, 2021

Lectio Divina for the Octave of Easter

We begin our prayer:

In the name of the Father, and of the Son, and of the Holy Spirit. Amen.

Almighty ever-living God,
who gave us the Paschal Mystery
in the covenant you established
for reconciling the human race,
so dispose our minds, we pray,
that what we celebrate by professing the faith
we may express in deeds.
Through our Lord Jesus Christ, your Son,
who lives and reigns with you in the unity of the Holy Spirit,
God, for ever and ever.

Collect, Friday within the Octave of Easter

Reading (*Lectio*)

Read the following Scripture two or three times.

Matthew 28:1-10

> After the sabbath, as the first day of the week was dawning, Mary Magdalene and the other Mary came to see the tomb. And behold, there was a great earthquake; for an angel of the Lord descended from heaven, approached, rolled back the stone, and sat upon it. His appearance was like lightning and his clothing was white as snow. The guards were shaken with fear of him and became like dead men. Then the angel said to the women in reply, "Do not be afraid! I know that you are seeking Jesus the crucified. He is not here, for he has been raised just as he said. Come and see the place where he lay. Then go quickly and tell his disciples, 'He has been raised from the dead, and he is going before you to Galilee; there you will see him.' Behold, I have told you." Then they went away quickly from the tomb, fearful yet overjoyed, and ran to announce this to his disciples. And behold, Jesus met them on their way and greeted them. They approached, embraced his feet, and did him homage. Then Jesus said to them, "Do not be afraid. Go tell my brothers to go to Galilee, and there they will see me."

Meditation (*Meditatio*)

After the reading, take some time to reflect in silence on one or more of the following questions:

- What word or words in this passage caught your attention?
- What in this passage comforted you?
- What in this passage challenged you?

If practicing lectio divina *as a family or in a group, after the reflection time, invite the participants to share their responses.*

Prayer (*Oratio*)

Read the scripture passage one more time. Bring to the Lord the praise, petition, or thanksgiving that the Word inspires in you.

Contemplation (*Contemplatio*)

Read the Scripture again, followed by this reflection:

≈ What conversion of mind, heart, and life is the Lord asking of me?

_____

_____

_____

_____

≈ *The guards were shaken with fear of him and became like dead men.* What makes me afraid and hesitant to do what is right? How does my faith strengthen me in spite of my fears and doubts?

_____

_____

_____

_____

≈ *He is not here, for he has been raised just as he said.* When have I relied on God's promises? How does God's Word give me strength in life's difficulties?

_____

_____

_____

_____

≈ *Then they went away quickly from the tomb, fearful yet overjoyed, and ran to announce this to his disciples.* When have I felt both fearful and overjoyed? How can I better share the wonder and awe that comes from faith in Christ?

_____

_____

_____

_____

≈ *After a period of silent reflection and/or discussion, all recite the Lord's Prayer and the following:*

Closing Prayer

Give thanks to the LORD, for he is good,
>   for his mercy endures forever.
Let the house of Israel say,
>   "His mercy endures forever."

"The right hand of the LORD has struck with power;
>   the right hand of the LORD is exalted.
I shall not die, but live,
>   and declare the works of the LORD."

The stone which the builders rejected
>   has become the cornerstone.
By the LORD has this been done;
>   it is wonderful in our eyes.

From Psalm 118

Living the Word This Week

How can I make my life a gift for others in charity?

Reach out to someone who is suffering from fear or doubt, either in person or by offering your prayers.

April 16, 2023

Lectio Divina for the Second Week of Easter

We begin our prayer:

In the name of the Father, and of the Son, and of the Holy Spirit. Amen.

O God, who willed that through the paschal mysteries
the gates of mercy should stand open for your faithful,
look upon us and have mercy,
that as we follow, by your gift, the way you desire for us,
so may we never stray from the paths of life.
Through our Lord Jesus Christ, your Son,
who lives and reigns with you in the unity of the Holy Spirit,
God, for ever and ever.

Collect, Saturday of the Second Week of Easter, second option

Reading (*Lectio*)

Read the following Scripture two or three times.

John 20:19-31

On the evening of that first day of the week, when the doors were locked, where the disciples were, for fear of the Jews, Jesus came and stood in their midst and said to them, "Peace be with you." When he had said this, he showed them his hands and his side. The disciples rejoiced when they saw the Lord. Jesus said to them again, "Peace be with you. As the Father has sent me, so I send you." And when he had said this, he breathed on them and said to them, "Receive the Holy Spirit. Whose sins you forgive are forgiven them, and whose sins you retain are retained."

Thomas, called Didymus, one of the Twelve, was not with them when Jesus came. So the other disciples said to him, "We have seen the Lord." But he said to them, "Unless I see the mark of the nails in his hands and put my finger into the nailmarks and put my hand into his side, I will not believe."

Now a week later his disciples were again inside and Thomas was with them. Jesus came, although the doors were locked, and stood in their midst and said, "Peace be with you." Then he said to Thomas, "Put your finger here and see my hands, and bring your hand and put it into my side, and do not be unbelieving, but believe." Thomas answered and said to him, "My Lord and my God!" Jesus said to him, "Have you come to believe because you have seen me? Blessed are those who have not seen and have believed."

Now Jesus did many other signs in the presence of his disciples that are not written in this book. But these are written that you may come to believe that Jesus is the Christ, the Son of God, and that through this belief you may have life in his name.

Meditation (*Meditatio*)

After the reading, take some time to reflect in silence on one or more of the following questions:

- What word or words in this passage caught your attention?
- What in this passage comforted you?
- What in this passage challenged you?

If practicing lectio divina *as a family or in a group, after the reflection time, invite the participants to share their responses.*

Prayer (*Oratio*)

Read the scripture passage one more time. Bring to the Lord the praise, petition, or thanksgiving that the Word inspires in you.

Contemplation (*Contemplatio*)

Read the Scripture again, followed by this reflection:

≈ What conversion of mind, heart, and life is the Lord asking of me?

_____

_____

_____

_____

~ *Peace be with you.* In what aspects of my life do I need to seek greater peace? How can I be a peacemaker in my family or community?

_____

_____

_____

_____

~ *As the Father has sent me, so I send you.* Where is God sending me? How can I respond more fully to his call?

_____

_____

_____

_____

~ *Do not be unbelieving, but believe.* What circumstances cause me to doubt or struggle in faith? What people or events strengthen my faith?

_____

_____

_____

_____

≈ *After a period of silent reflection and/or discussion, all recite the Lord's Prayer and the following:*

Closing Prayer

Let the house of Israel say,
    "His mercy endures forever."
Let the house of Aaron say,
    "His mercy endures forever."
Let those who fear the LORD say,
    "His mercy endures forever."

I was hard pressed and was falling,
    but the LORD helped me.
My strength and my courage is the LORD,
    and he has been my savior.
The joyful shout of victory
    in the tents of the just:

The stone which the builders rejected
    has become the cornerstone.
By the LORD has this been done;
    it is wonderful in our eyes.
This is the day the LORD has made;
    let us be glad and rejoice in it.

From Psalm 118

Living the Word This Week

How can I make my life a gift for others in charity?

Pray for peace in your community and in the world and prayerfully consider participating in the peace efforts of your parish or diocese.

April 23, 2023

Lectio Divina for the Third Week of Easter

We begin our prayer:

In the name of the Father, and of the Son, and of the Holy Spirit. Amen.

Grant, we pray, almighty God,
that we, who have come to know
the grace of the Lord's Resurrection,
may, through the love of the Spirit,
ourselves rise to newness of life.
Through our Lord Jesus Christ, your Son,
who lives and reigns with you in the unity of the Holy Spirit,
God, for ever and ever.

Collect, Friday of the Third Week of Easter

Reading (*Lectio*)

Read the following Scripture two or three times.

Luke 24:13-35

That very day, the first day of the week, two of Jesus' disciples were going to a village seven miles from Jerusalem called Emmaus, and they were conversing about all the things that had occurred. And it happened that while they were conversing and debating, Jesus himself drew near and walked with them, but their eyes were prevented from recognizing him. He asked them, "What are you discussing as you walk along?" They stopped, looking downcast. One of them, named Cleopas, said to him in reply, "Are you the only visitor to Jerusalem who does not know of the things that have taken place there in these days?" And he replied to them, "What sort of things?" They said to him, "The things that happened to Jesus the Nazarene, who was a prophet mighty in deed and word before God and all the people, how our chief priests and rulers both handed him over to a sentence of death and crucified him. But we were hoping that he would be the one to redeem Israel; and besides all this, it is now the third day since this took place. Some women from our group, however, have astounded us: they were at the tomb early in the morning and did not find his body; they came back and reported that they had indeed seen a vision of angels who announced that he was alive. Then some of those with us went to the tomb and found things just as the women had described, but him they did not see." And he said to them, "Oh, how foolish you are! How slow of heart to believe all that the prophets spoke! Was it not necessary that the Christ should suffer these things and enter into his glory?" Then beginning with Moses and all the prophets, he interpreted to them what referred to him in all the Scriptures. As they approached the village to which they were going, he gave the impression that he was going on farther. But they urged him, "Stay with us, for it is nearly evening and the day is almost over." So he went in to stay with them. And it happened that, while he was with them at table, he took bread, said the blessing, broke it, and gave it to them. With that their eyes were opened and they recognized him, but he vanished from their sight. Then they said to each other, "Were not our hearts burning within us while he spoke to us on the way and opened the Scriptures to us?" So they set out at once and returned to Jerusalem where they found gathered together the eleven and those with them who were saying, "The Lord has truly been raised and has appeared to Simon!" Then the two recounted what had taken place on the way and how he was made known to them in the breaking of bread.

Meditation (*Meditatio*)

After the reading, take some time to reflect in silence on one or more of the following questions:

- What word or words in this passage caught your attention?
- What in this passage comforted you?
- What in this passage challenged you?

If practicing lectio divina *as a family or in a group, after the reflection time, invite the participants to share their responses.*

Prayer (*Oratio*)

Read the scripture passage one more time. Bring to the Lord the praise, petition, or thanksgiving that the Word inspires in you.

Contemplation (*Contemplatio*)

Read the Scripture again, followed by this reflection:

≈ What conversion of mind, heart, and life is the Lord asking of me?

_____

_____

_____

_____

≈ *They were conversing about all the things that had occurred.* How can I make my words kinder and more charitable? When is the last time I discussed my faith with someone?

_____

_____

_____

_____

≈ *Was it not necessary that the Christ should suffer these things and enter into his glory?* What suffering is God asking me to bear right now? How can I see Christ in those who are suffering?

_____

_____

_____

_____

≈ *He was made known to them in the breaking of bread.* How do I demonstrate my faith in and love for the Holy Eucharist? What fruits do I receive in attending Mass?

_____

_____

_____

_____

≈ *After a period of silent reflection and/or discussion, all recite the Lord's Prayer and the following:*

Closing Prayer

Keep me, O God, for in you I take refuge;
    I say to the LORD, "My Lord are you."
O LORD, my allotted portion and my cup,
    you it is who hold fast my lot.

I bless the LORD who counsels me;
    even in the night my heart exhorts me.
I set the LORD ever before me;
    with him at my right hand I shall not be disturbed.

Therefore my heart is glad and my soul rejoices,
   my body, too, abides in confidence;
because you will not abandon my soul to the netherworld,
   nor will you suffer your faithful one to undergo corruption.

You will show me the path to life,
   abounding joy in your presence,
      the delights at your right hand forever.

From Psalm 16

Living the Word This Week

How can I make my life a gift for others in charity?

Spend some time praying before the Blessed Sacrament or reflecting on the resources available at www.eucharisticrevival.org.

April 30, 2023

Lectio Divina for the Fourth Week of Easter

We begin our prayer:

In the name of the Father, and of the Son, and of the Holy Spirit. Amen.

O God, life of the faithful,
glory of the humble, blessedness of the just,
listen kindly to the prayers
of those who call on you,
that they who thirst for what you generously promise
may always have their fill of your plenty.
Through our Lord Jesus Christ, your Son,
who lives and reigns with you in the unity of the Holy Spirit,
God, for ever and ever.

Collect, Wednesday of the Fourth Week of Easter

Reading (*Lectio*)

Read the following Scripture two or three times.

John 10:1-10

Jesus said: "Amen, amen, I say to you, whoever does not enter a sheepfold through the gate but climbs over elsewhere is a thief and a robber. But whoever enters through the gate is the shepherd of the sheep. The gatekeeper opens it for him, and the sheep hear his voice, as the shepherd calls his own sheep by name and leads them out. When he has driven out all his own, he walks ahead of them, and the sheep follow him, because they recognize his voice. But they will not follow a stranger; they will run away from him, because they do not recognize the voice of strangers." Although Jesus used this figure of speech, the Pharisees did not realize what he was trying to tell them.

So Jesus said again, "Amen, amen, I say to you, I am the gate for the sheep. All who came before me are thieves and robbers, but the sheep did not listen to them. I am the gate. Whoever enters through me will be saved, and will come in and go out and find pasture. A thief comes only to steal and slaughter and destroy; I came so that they might have life and have it more abundantly."

Meditation (*Meditatio*)

After the reading, take some time to reflect in silence on one or more of the following questions:

- What word or words in this passage caught your attention?
- What in this passage comforted you?
- What in this passage challenged you?

If practicing lectio divina *as a family or in a group, after the reflection time, invite the participants to share their responses.*

Prayer (*Oratio*)

Read the scripture passage one more time. Bring to the Lord the praise, petition, or thanksgiving that the Word inspires in you.

Contemplation (*Contemplatio*)

Read the Scripture again, followed by this reflection:

≈ What conversion of mind, heart, and life is the Lord asking of me?

_____

_____

_____

_____

≈ *He walks ahead of them, and the sheep follow him, because they recognize his voice.* How do I recognize the voice of God? Where is Jesus calling me to follow him?

_____

_____

_____

_____

∼ *But they will not follow a stranger; they will run away from him, because they do not recognize the voice of strangers.* What strange and divisive voices pull me away from God? How can I mute those voices?

_____

_____

_____

_____

∼ *Whoever enters through me will be saved, and will come in and go out and find pasture.* Where do I find pasture and rest? What opportunities for rest and restoration are available to me?

_____

_____

_____

_____

∼ *After a period of silent reflection and/or discussion, all recite the Lord's Prayer and the following:*

Closing Prayer

The Lord is my shepherd; I shall not want.
    In verdant pastures he gives me repose;
beside restful waters he leads me;
    he refreshes my soul.

He guides me in right paths
   for his name's sake.
Even though I walk in the dark valley
   I fear no evil; for you are at my side.
With your rod and your staff
   that give me courage.

You spread the table before me
   in the sight of my foes;
you anoint my head with oil;
   my cup overflows.

Only goodness and kindness follow me
   all the days of my life;
and I shall dwell in the house of the LORD
   for years to come.

From Psalm 23

Living the Word This Week

How can I make my life a gift for others in charity?

Pray for the Pope and the bishops who are called to shepherd God's
people.

May 7, 2023

Lectio Divina for the Fifth Week of Easter

We begin our prayer:

In the name of the Father, and of the Son, and of the Holy Spirit. Amen.

O God, by whose grace,
though sinners, we are made just
and, though pitiable, made blessed,
stand, we pray, by your works,
stand by your gifts,
that those justified by faith
may not lack the courage of perseverance.
Through our Lord Jesus Christ, your Son,
who lives and reigns with you in the unity of the Holy Spirit,
God, for ever and ever.

Collect, Thursday of the Fifth Week of Easter

Reading (*Lectio*)

Read the following Scripture two or three times.

John 14:1-12

> Jesus said to his disciples: "Do not let your hearts be troubled. You have faith in God; have faith also in me. In my Father's house there are many dwelling places. If there were not, would I have told you that I am going to prepare a place for you? And if I go and prepare a place for you, I will come back again and take you to myself, so that where I am you also may be. Where I am going you know the way." Thomas said to him, "Master, we do not know where you are going; how can we know the way?" Jesus said to him, "I am the way and the truth and the life. No one comes to the Father except through me. If you know me, then you will also know my Father. From now on you do know him and have seen him." Philip said to him, "Master, show us the Father, and that will be enough for us." Jesus said to him, "Have I been with you for so long a time and you still do not know me, Philip? Whoever has seen me has seen the Father. How can you say, 'Show us the Father'? Do you not believe that I am in the Father and the Father is in me? The words that I speak to you I do not speak on my own. The Father who dwells in me is doing his works. Believe me that I am in the Father and the Father is in me, or else, believe because of the works themselves. Amen, amen, I say to you, whoever believes in me will do the works that I do, and will do greater ones than these, because I am going to the Father."

Meditation (*Meditatio*)

After the reading, take some time to reflect in silence on one or more of the following questions:

- What word or words in this passage caught your attention?
- What in this passage comforted you?
- What in this passage challenged you?

If practicing lectio divina *as a family or in a group, after the reflection time, invite the participants to share their responses.*

Prayer (*Oratio*)

Read the scripture passage one more time. Bring to the Lord the praise, petition, or thanksgiving that the Word inspires in you.

Contemplation (*Contemplatio*)

Read the Scripture again, followed by this reflection:

∾ What conversion of mind, heart, and life is the Lord asking of me?

_____

_____

_____

_____

≈ *I will come back again and take you to myself, so that where I am you also may be.* When have I felt that God is far away from me? When have I felt that God is near?

_____

_____

_____

_____

≈ *If you know me, then you will also know my Father.* How can I get to know God better? How can I grow in love for God and his Church?

_____

_____

_____

_____

≈ *Believe because of the works themselves.* How do I demonstrate my faith by the way I live? How can I be of greater service to those in need?

_____

_____

_____

_____

~ After a period of silent reflection and/or discussion, all recite the Lord's Prayer and the following:

Closing Prayer

> Exult, you just, in the LORD;
> > praise from the upright is fitting.
> Give thanks to the LORD on the harp;
> > with the ten-stringed lyre chant his praises.
>
> Upright is the word of the LORD,
> > and all his works are trustworthy.
> He loves justice and right;
> > of the kindness of the LORD the earth is full.
>
> See, the eyes of the LORD are upon those who fear him,
> > upon those who hope for his kindness,
> To deliver them from death
> > and preserve them in spite of famine.

From Psalm 33

Living the Word This Week

How can I make my life a gift for others in charity?

Learn more about Catholic social teaching (https://www.usccb.org/offices/justice-peace-human-development/catholic-social-teaching) as a way to put your faith into practice.

May 14, 2023

Lectio Divina for the Sixth Week of Easter

We begin our prayer:

In the name of the Father, and of the Son, and of the Holy Spirit. Amen.

Grant, we pray, O Lord,
that, as we celebrate in mystery
the solemnities of your Son's Resurrection,
so, too, we may be worthy
to rejoice at his coming with all the Saints.
Through our Lord Jesus Christ, your Son,
who lives and reigns with you in the unity of the Holy Spirit,
God, for ever and ever.

Collect, Wednesday of the Sixth Week of Easter, Morning Mass

Reading (*Lectio*)

Read the following Scripture two or three times.

John 14:15-21

> Jesus said to his disciples: "If you love me, you will keep my commandments. And I will ask the Father, and he will give you another Advocate to be with you always, the Spirit of truth, whom the world cannot accept, because it neither sees nor knows him. But you know him, because he remains with you, and will be in you. I will not leave you orphans; I will come to you. In a little while the world will no longer see me, but you will see me, because I live and you will live. On that day you will realize that I am in my Father and you are in me and I in you. Whoever has my commandments and observes them is the one who loves me. And whoever loves me will be loved by my Father, and I will love him and reveal myself to him."

Meditation (*Meditatio*)

After the reading, take some time to reflect in silence on one or more of the following questions:

- What word or words in this passage caught your attention?
- What in this passage comforted you?
- What in this passage challenged you?

If practicing lectio divina *as a family or in a group, after the reflection time, invite the participants to share their responses.*

Prayer (*Oratio*)

Read the scripture passage one more time. Bring to the Lord the praise, petition, or thanksgiving that the Word inspires in you.

Contemplation (*Contemplatio*)

Read the Scripture again, followed by this reflection:

≈ What conversion of mind, heart, and life is the Lord asking of me?

_____

_____

_____

_____

≈ *The Spirit of truth, whom the world cannot accept, because it neither sees nor knows him.* When have I failed to give witness to God's truth? What can I do to help create a more just and truth-filled culture?

_____

_____

_____

_____

∼ *Whoever has my commandments and observes them is the one who loves me.* Which commandments of the Lord do I struggle to observe? How do I demonstrate my love for Jesus through my actions?

_____

_____

_____

_____

∼ *I will love him and reveal myself to him.* How has God revealed himself to me this week? How can I help others to perceive God's actions in their lives?

_____

_____

_____

_____

∼ *After a period of silent reflection and/or discussion, all recite the Lord's Prayer and the following:*

Closing Prayer

Shout joyfully to God, all the earth,
    sing praise to the glory of his name;
    proclaim his glorious praise.
Say to God, "How tremendous are your deeds!"

"Let all on earth worship and sing praise to you,
    sing praise to your name!"
Come and see the works of God,
    his tremendous deeds among the children of Adam.

He has changed the sea into dry land;
    through the river they passed on foot;
    therefore let us rejoice in him.
He rules by his might forever.

Hear now, all you who fear God, while I declare
    what he has done for me.
Blessed be God who refused me not
    my prayer or his kindness!

From Psalm 66

Living the Word This Week

How can I make my life a gift for others in charity?

Learn more about developing greater civility in politics and society: https://ww.usccb.org/civilizeit

May 18, 2023

Lectio Divina for the Solemnity of the Ascension

We begin our prayer:

In the name of the Father, and of the Son, and of the Holy Spirit. Amen.

Gladden us with holy joys, almighty God,
and make us rejoice with devout thanksgiving,
for the Ascension of Christ your Son
is our exaltation,
and, where the Head has gone before in glory,
the Body is called to follow in hope.
Through our Lord Jesus Christ, your Son,
who lives and reigns with you in the unity of the Holy Spirit,
God, for ever and ever.

Collect, Ascension, Mass during the Day

Reading (*Lectio*)

Read the following Scripture two or three times.

Matthew 28:16-20

> The eleven disciples went to Galilee, to the mountain to which Jesus had ordered them. When they saw him, they worshiped, but they doubted. Then Jesus approached and said to them, "All power in heaven and on earth has been given to me. Go, therefore, and make disciples of all nations, baptizing them in the name of the Father, and of the Son, and of the Holy Spirit, teaching them to observe all that I have commanded you. And behold, I am with you always, until the end of the age."

Meditation (*Meditatio*)

After the reading, take some time to reflect in silence on one or more of the following questions:

- What word or words in this passage caught your attention?
- What in this passage comforted you?
- What in this passage challenged you?

If practicing lectio divina *as a family or in a group, after the reflection time, invite the participants to share their responses.*

Prayer (*Oratio*)

Read the scripture passage one more time. Bring to the Lord the praise, petition, or thanksgiving that the Word inspires in you.

Contemplation (*Contemplatio*)

Read the Scripture again, followed by this reflection:

∾ What conversion of mind, heart, and life is the Lord asking of me?

_____

_____

_____

_____

∾ *The eleven disciples went to Galilee, to the mountain to which Jesus had ordered them.* How do I discern God's will for me? How can I become more docile to that will?

_____

_____

_____

_____

∾ *All power in heaven and on earth has been given to me.* How have I experienced God's power and majesty? How can I respond in adoration and thanksgiving to all that God has done for me?

_____

_____

_____

_____

≈ *Go, therefore, and make disciples of all nations.* When was the last time I shared my faith with someone? How can I develop an evangelizing spirit?

_____

_____

_____

_____

≈ *After a period of silent reflection and/or discussion, all recite the Lord's Prayer and the following:*

Closing Prayer

All you peoples, clap your hands,
    shout to God with cries of gladness,
For the LORD, the Most High, the awesome,
    is the great king over all the earth.

God mounts his throne amid shouts of joy;
    the LORD, amid trumpet blasts.
Sing praise to God, sing praise;
    sing praise to our king, sing praise.

For king of all the earth is God;
    sing hymns of praise.
God reigns over the nations,
    God sits upon his holy throne.

From Psalm 47

Living the Word This Week

How can I make my life a gift for others in charity?

Learn more about evangelization by reading the vision of *Go and Make Disciples*: https://www.usccb.org/beliefs-and-teachings/how-we-teach/evangelization/go-and-make-disciples/go-and-make-disciples-a-national-plan-and-strategy-for-catholic-evangelization-in-the-united-states

May 21, 2023

Lectio Divina for the Seventh Week of Easter

We begin our prayer:

In the name of the Father, and of the Son, and of the Holy Spirit. Amen.

May the power of the Holy Spirit
come to us, we pray, O Lord,
that we may keep your will faithfully in mind
and express it in a devout way of life.
Through our Lord Jesus Christ, your Son,
who lives and reigns with you in the unity of the Holy Spirit,
God, for ever and ever.

Collect, Monday of the Seventh Week of Easter

Reading (*Lectio*)

Read the following Scripture two or three times.

John 17:1-11a

> Jesus raised his eyes to heaven and said, "Father, the hour has come. Give glory to your son, so that your son may glorify you, just as you gave him authority over all people, so that your son may give eternal life to all you gave him. Now this is eternal life, that they should know you, the only true God, and the one whom you sent, Jesus Christ. I glorified you on earth by accomplishing the work that you gave me to do. Now glorify me, Father, with you, with the glory that I had with you before the world began.
>
> "I revealed your name to those whom you gave me out of the world. They belonged to you, and you gave them to me, and they have kept your word. Now they know that everything you gave me is from you, because the words you gave to me I have given to them, and they accepted them and truly understood that I came from you, and they have believed that you sent me. I pray for them. I do not pray for the world but for the ones you have given me, because they are yours, and everything of mine is yours and everything of yours is mine, and I have been glorified in them. And now I will no longer be in the world, but they are in the world, while I am coming to you."

Meditation (*Meditatio*)

After the reading, take some time to reflect in silence on one or more of the following questions:

- What word or words in this passage caught your attention?
- What in this passage comforted you?
- What in this passage challenged you?

If practicing lectio divina *as a family or in a group, after the reflection time, invite the participants to share their responses.*

Prayer (*Oratio*)

Read the scripture passage one more time. Bring to the Lord the praise, petition, or thanksgiving that the Word inspires in you.

Contemplation (*Contemplatio*)

Read the Scripture again, followed by this reflection:

≈ What conversion of mind, heart, and life is the Lord asking of me?

_____

_____

_____

_____

≈ *Father, the hour has come.* How much time do I commit to my faith? How can I orient my daily life so that God is its center?

_____

_____

_____

_____

≈ *I glorified you on earth by accomplishing the work that you gave me to do.* How can I glorify God by my life? Whose faithful life inspires me?

_____

_____

_____

_____

≈ *I pray for them.* Who has asked me to pray for them? What needs do I bring to prayer today?

_____

_____

_____

_____

~ *After a period of silent reflection and/or discussion, all recite the Lord's Prayer and the following:*

Closing Prayer

The LORD is my light and my salvation;
    whom should I fear?
The LORD is my life's refuge;
    of whom should I be afraid?

One thing I ask of the LORD;
    this I seek:
To dwell in the house of the LORD
    all the days of my life,
That I may gaze on the loveliness of the LORD
    and contemplate his temple.

Hear, O LORD, the sound of my call;
    have pity on me, and answer me.
Of you my heart speaks; you my glance seeks.

From Psalm 27

Living the Word This Week

How can I make my life a gift for others in charity?

Review your weekly schedule/calendar to determine how you can increase time for prayer, liturgy, study, and service.

May 28, 2023

Lectio Divina for the Solemnity of Pentecost

We begin our prayer:

In the name of the Father, and of the Son, and of the Holy Spirit. Amen.

O God, who by the mystery of today's great feast
sanctify your whole Church in every people and nation,
pour out, we pray, the gifts of the Holy Spirit
across the face of the earth
and, with the divine grace that was at work
when the Gospel was first proclaimed,
fill now once more the hearts of believers.
Through our Lord Jesus Christ, your Son,
who lives and reigns with you in the unity of the Holy Spirit,
God, for ever and ever.

Collect, Pentecost, Mass during the Day

Reading (*Lectio*)

Read the following Scripture two or three times.

John 20:19-23

> On the evening of that first day of the week, when the doors were
> locked, where the disciples were, for fear of the Jews, Jesus came
> and stood in their midst and said to them, "Peace be with you."
> When he had said this, he showed them his hands and his side.
> The disciples rejoiced when they saw the Lord. Jesus said to them
> again, "Peace be with you. As the Father has sent me, so I send
> you." And when he had said this, he breathed on them and said
> to them, "Receive the Holy Spirit. Whose sins you forgive are for-
> given them, and whose sins you retain are retained."

Meditation (*Meditatio*)

*After the reading, take some time to reflect in silence on one or more of the
following questions:*

- What word or words in this passage caught your attention?
- What in this passage comforted you?
- What in this passage challenged you?

If practicing lectio divina *as a family or in a group, after the reflection
time, invite the participants to share their responses.*

Prayer (*Oratio*)

*Read the scripture passage one more time. Bring to the Lord the praise, pe-
tition, or thanksgiving that the Word inspires in you.*

Contemplation (*Contemplatio*)

Read the Scripture again, followed by this reflection:

∼ What conversion of mind, heart, and life is the Lord asking of me?

_____

_____

_____

_____

∼ *When the doors were locked.* How have I locked the doors of my heart against those who need my love? How have I refused to share my time, treasure, talent, and love?

_____

_____

_____

_____

∼ *Jesus came and stood in their midst.* When do I feel closest to Jesus? How can I learn to see Jesus in other people, especially the marginalized?

_____

_____

＿＿＿＿＿＿＿＿＿＿＿＿＿＿＿＿＿＿＿＿＿＿＿＿＿＿＿＿＿

＿＿＿＿＿＿＿＿＿＿＿＿＿＿＿＿＿＿＿＿＿＿＿＿＿＿＿＿＿

～ *Receive the Holy Spirit.* What gifts have I received from the Holy
Spirit? How can I place these gifts at the service of the community?

＿＿＿＿＿＿＿＿＿＿＿＿＿＿＿＿＿＿＿＿＿＿＿＿＿＿＿＿＿

＿＿＿＿＿＿＿＿＿＿＿＿＿＿＿＿＿＿＿＿＿＿＿＿＿＿＿＿＿

＿＿＿＿＿＿＿＿＿＿＿＿＿＿＿＿＿＿＿＿＿＿＿＿＿＿＿＿＿

＿＿＿＿＿＿＿＿＿＿＿＿＿＿＿＿＿＿＿＿＿＿＿＿＿＿＿＿＿

～ After a period of silent reflection and/or discussion, all recite the
Lord's Prayer and the following:

Closing Prayer

Bless the LORD, O my soul!
 O LORD, my God, you are great indeed!
How manifold are your works, O LORD!
 the earth is full of your creatures;

If you take away their breath, they perish
 and return to their dust.
When you send forth your spirit, they are created,
 and you renew the face of the earth.

May the glory of the Lord endure forever;
    may the Lord be glad in his works!
Pleasing to him be my theme;
    I will be glad in the Lord.

From Psalm 104

Living the Word This Week

How can I make my life a gift for others in charity?

Join a diocesan, state, or national advocacy effort to speak out on behalf of the underprivileged and voiceless.

June 4, 2023

Lectio Divina for the Solemnity of the Most Holy Trinity

We begin our prayer:

In the name of the Father, and of the Son, and of the Holy Spirit. Amen.

God our Father, who by sending into the world
the Word of truth and the Spirit of sanctification
made known to the human race your wondrous mystery,
grant us, we pray, that in professing the true faith,
we may acknowledge the Trinity of eternal glory
and adore your Unity, powerful in majesty.
Through our Lord Jesus Christ, your Son,
who lives and reigns with you in the unity of the Holy Spirit,
God, for ever and ever.

Collect, Solemnity of the Most Holy Trinity

Reading (*Lectio*)

Read the following Scripture two or three times.

John 3:16-18

> God so loved the world that he gave his only Son, so that everyone who believes in him might not perish but might have eternal life. For God did not send his Son into the world to condemn the world, but that the world might be saved through him. Whoever believes in him will not be condemned, but whoever does not believe has already been condemned, because he has not believed in the name of the only Son of God.

Meditation (*Meditatio*)

After the reading, take some time to reflect in silence on one or more of the following questions:

- What word or words in this passage caught your attention?
- What in this passage comforted you?
- What in this passage challenged you?

If practicing lectio divina *as a family or in a group, after the reflection time, invite the participants to share their responses.*

Prayer (*Oratio*)

Read the scripture passage one more time. Bring to the Lord the praise, petition, or thanksgiving that the Word inspires in you.

Contemplation (*Contemplatio*)

Read the Scripture again, followed by this reflection:

∾ What conversion of mind, heart, and life is the Lord asking of me?

_____

_____

_____

_____

∾ *God so loved the world that he gave his only Son.* How can I follow Jesus' example by giving of myself? How can I express my love for all that God has created?

_____

_____

_____

_____

∾ *So that everyone who believes in him might not perish but might have eternal life.* What do I imagine that heaven will be like? How am I preparing for eternal life with God?

_____

_____

_____

~ *Whoever believes in him will not be condemned.* How often do I judge or condemn others? How can accompany others instead of judging them?

_____

_____

_____

_____

~ *After a period of silent reflection and/or discussion, all recite the Lord's Prayer and the following:*

Closing Prayer

Blessed are you, O Lord, the God of our fathers,
    praiseworthy and exalted above all forever;
And blessed is your holy and glorious name,
    praiseworthy and exalted above all for all ages.

Blessed are you in the temple of your holy glory,
    praiseworthy and glorious above all forever.

Blessed are you on the throne of your kingdom,
    praiseworthy and exalted above all forever.

Blessed are you who look into the depths
from your throne upon the cherubim,
praiseworthy and exalted above all forever.

From Daniel 3

Living the Word This Week

How can I make my life a gift for others in charity?

Visit a cemetery and pray for those who have died or pray for the grace of a happy death.

June 11, 2023

Lectio Divina for the Solemnity of the Most Holy Body and Blood of Christ (*Corpus Christi*)

We begin our prayer:

In the name of the Father, and of the Son, and of the Holy Spirit. Amen.

O God, who in this wonderful Sacrament
have left us a memorial of your Passion,
grant us, we pray,
so to revere the sacred mysteries of your Body and Blood
that we may always experience in ourselves
the fruits of your redemption.
Who live and reign with God the Father
in the unity of the Holy Spirit,
God, for ever and ever.

Collect, Solemnity of the Most Holy Body and Blood of Christ

Reading (*Lectio*)

Read the following Scripture two or three times.

John 6:51-58

> Jesus said to the Jewish crowds: "I am the living bread that came down from heaven; whoever eats this bread will live forever; and the bread that I will give is my flesh for the life of the world."

> The Jews quarreled among themselves, saying, "How can this man give us his flesh to eat?" Jesus said to them, "Amen, amen, I say to you, unless you eat the flesh of the Son of Man and drink his blood, you do not have life within you. Whoever eats my flesh and drinks my blood has eternal life, and I will raise him on the last day. For my flesh is true food, and my blood is true drink. Whoever eats my flesh and drinks my blood remains in me and I in him. Just as the living Father sent me and I have life because of the Father, so also the one who feeds on me will have life because of me. This is the bread that came down from heaven. Unlike your ancestors who ate and still died, whoever eats this bread will live forever."

Meditation (*Meditatio*)

After the reading, take some time to reflect in silence on one or more of the following questions:

- What word or words in this passage caught your attention?
- What in this passage comforted you?
- What in this passage challenged you?

If practicing lectio divina *as a family or in a group, after the reflection time, invite the participants to share their responses.*

Prayer (*Oratio*)

Read the scripture passage one more time. Bring to the Lord the praise, petition, or thanksgiving that the Word inspires in you.

Contemplation (*Contemplatio*)

Read the Scripture again, followed by this reflection:

≈ What conversion of mind, heart, and life is the Lord asking of me?

_____

_____

_____

_____

≈ *The bread that I will give is my flesh for the life of the world.* How is my faith nourished? How do I help others nourish their faith?

_____

_____

_____

_____

≈ *The Jews quarreled among themselves.* What signs of division do I see in my family, parish, or community? How can I be a peacemaker in the communities where I live and work?

_____

_____

_____

_____

≈ *Whoever eats my flesh and drinks my blood remains in me and I in him.* What can I do this week to grow closer to Jesus? How can I receive the Eucharist with greater devotion?

_____

_____

_____

_____

≈ *After a period of silent reflection and/or discussion, all recite the Lord's Prayer and the following:*

Closing Prayer

Glorify the LORD, O Jerusalem;
　　praise your God, O Zion.
For he has strengthened the bars of your gates;
　　he has blessed your children within you.

He has granted peace in your borders;
    with the best of wheat he fills you.
He sends forth his command to the earth;
    swiftly runs his word!

He has proclaimed his word to Jacob,
    his statutes and his ordinances to Israel.
He has not done thus for any other nation;
    his ordinances he has not made known to them. Alleluia.

From Psalm 147

Living the Word This Week

How can I make my life a gift for others in charity?

Spend an hour in prayer before the Blessed Sacrament.

June 16, 2023

Lectio Divina for the Solemnity of the Sacred Heart

We begin our prayer:

In the name of the Father, and of the Son, and of the Holy Spirit. Amen.

Grant, we pray, almighty God,
that we, who glory in the Heart of your beloved Son
and recall the wonders of his love for us,
may be made worthy to receive
an overflowing measure of grace
from that fount of heavenly gifts.
Through our Lord Jesus Christ, your Son,
who lives and reigns with you in the unity of the Holy Spirit,
God, for ever and ever.

Collect, Solemnity of the Sacred Heart, first option

Reading (*Lectio*)

Read the following Scripture two or three times.

Matthew 11:25-30

> At that time Jesus exclaimed: "I give praise to you, Father, Lord of heaven and earth, for although you have hidden these things from the wise and the learned you have revealed them to little ones. Yes, Father, such has been your gracious will. All things have been handed over to me by my Father. No one knows the Son except the Father, and no one knows the Father except the Son and anyone to whom the Son wishes to reveal him.
>
> "Come to me, all you who labor and are burdened, and I will give you rest. Take my yoke upon you and learn from me, for I am meek and humble of heart; and you will find rest for yourselves. For my yoke is easy, and my burden light."

Meditation (*Meditatio*)

After the reading, take some time to reflect in silence on one or more of the following questions:

- What word or words in this passage caught your attention?
- What in this passage comforted you?
- What in this passage challenged you?

If practicing lectio divina *as a family or in a group, after the reflection time, invite the participants to share their responses.*

Prayer (*Oratio*)

Read the scripture passage one more time. Bring to the Lord the praise, petition, or thanksgiving that the Word inspires in you.

Contemplation (*Contemplatio*)

Read the Scripture again, followed by this reflection:

≈ What conversion of mind, heart, and life is the Lord asking of me?

_____

_____

_____

_____

≈ *I give praise to you, Father, Lord of heaven and earth.* What shall I praise God for today? How do I see God's hand in creation, our common home?

_____

_____

_____

_____

~ *Although you have hidden these things from the wise and the learned you have revealed them to little ones.* How has my faith changed as I have grown older? How can I nurture a spirit of simplicity and humility?

_____

_____

_____

_____

~ *Take my yoke upon you and learn from me.* What burdens is God asking me to bear? How can I join my sufferings to those of Christ?

_____

_____

_____

_____

~ *After a period of silent reflection and/or discussion, all recite the Lord's Prayer and the following:*

Closing Prayer

Bless the LORD, O my soul;
    all my being, bless his holy name.
Bless the LORD, O my soul;
    and forget not all his benefits.

He pardons all your iniquities,
    heals all your ills.
He redeems your life from destruction,
    crowns you with kindness and compassion.

Merciful and gracious is the LORD,
    slow to anger and abounding in kindness.
Not according to our sins does he deal with us,
    nor does he requite us according to our crimes.

From Psalm 103

Living the Word This Week

How can I make my life a gift for others in charity?

Read Chapter 2 of *Laudato Si': On Care for Our Common Home*:
www.vatican.va/content/francesco/en/encyclicals/documents/
papa-francesco_20150524_enciclica-laudato-si.html

June 18, 2023

Lectio Divina for the Eleventh Week in Ordinary Time

We begin our prayer:

In the name of the Father, and of the Son, and of the Holy Spirit. Amen.

O God, strength of those who hope in you,
graciously hear our pleas,
and, since without you mortal frailty can do nothing,
grant us always the help of your grace,
that in following your commands
we may please you by our resolve and our deeds.
Through our Lord Jesus Christ, your Son,
who lives and reigns with you in the unity of the Holy Spirit,
God, for ever and ever.

Collect, Eleventh Sunday in Ordinary Time

Reading (*Lectio*)

Read the following Scripture two or three times.

Matthew 9:36—10:8

At the sight of the crowds, Jesus' heart was moved with pity for them because they were troubled and abandoned, like sheep without a shepherd. Then he said to his disciples, "The harvest is abundant but the laborers are few; so ask the master of the harvest to send out laborers for his harvest."

Then he summoned his twelve disciples and gave them authority over unclean spirits to drive them out and to cure every disease and every illness. The names of the twelve apostles are these: first, Simon called Peter, and his brother Andrew; James, the son of Zebedee, and his brother John; Philip and Bartholomew, Thomas and Matthew the tax collector; James, the son of Alphaeus, and Thaddeus; Simon from Cana, and Judas Iscariot who betrayed him.

Jesus sent out these twelve after instructing them thus, "Do not go into pagan territory or enter a Samaritan town. Go rather to the lost sheep of the house of Israel. As you go, make this proclamation: 'The kingdom of heaven is at hand.' Cure the sick, raise the dead, cleanse lepers, drive out demons. Without cost you have received; without cost you are to give."

Meditation (*Meditatio*)

After the reading, take some time to reflect in silence on one or more of the following questions:

- What word or words in this passage caught your attention?
- What in this passage comforted you?
- What in this passage challenged you?

If practicing lectio divina *as a family or in a group, after the reflection time, invite the participants to share their responses.*

Prayer (*Oratio*)

Read the scripture passage one more time. Bring to the Lord the praise, petition, or thanksgiving that the Word inspires in you.

Contemplation (*Contemplatio*)

Read the Scripture again, followed by this reflection:

~ What conversion of mind, heart, and life is the Lord asking of me?

_____

_____

_____

_____

≈ *Jesus' heart was moved with pity for them because they were troubled and abandoned, like sheep without a shepherd.* When have I felt troubled and abandoned? How can I be more attentive to those on the margins who feel as though no one cares?

_____

_____

_____

_____

≈ *The harvest is abundant but the laborers are few.* What fruits do I reap from the practice of my faith? How can I better serve God and my neighbors?

_____

_____

_____

_____

≈ *Without cost you have received; without cost you are to give.* What gifts has God given to me? How can I express my gratitude for these gifts?

_____

_____

_____

_____

~ After a period of silent reflection and/or discussion, all recite the Lord's Prayer and the following:

Closing Prayer

Sing joyfully to the LORD, all you lands;
> serve the LORD with gladness;
> come before him with joyful song.

Know that the LORD is God;
> he made us, his we are;
> his people, the flock he tends.

The LORD is good:
> his kindness endures forever,
> and his faithfulness to all generations.

From Psalm 100

Living the Word This Week

How can I make my life a gift for others in charity?

Pray for an increase in vocations to the priesthood, diaconate, and consecrated life.

June 25, 2023

Lectio Divina for the Twelfth Week in Ordinary Time

We begin our prayer:

In the name of the Father, and of the Son, and of the Holy Spirit. Amen.

Grant, O Lord,
that we may always revere and love your holy name,
for you never deprive of your guidance
those you set firm on the foundation of your love.
Through our Lord Jesus Christ, your Son,
who lives and reigns with you in the unity of the Holy Spirit,
God, for ever and ever.

Collect, Twelfth Sunday in Ordinary Time

Reading (*Lectio*)

Read the following Scripture two or three times.

Matthew 10:26-33

> Jesus said to the Twelve: "Fear no one. Nothing is concealed that will not be revealed, nor secret that will not be known. What I say to you in the darkness, speak in the light; what you hear whispered, proclaim on the housetops. And do not be afraid of those who kill the body but cannot kill the soul; rather, be afraid of the one who can destroy both soul and body in Gehenna. Are not two sparrows sold for a small coin? Yet not one of them falls to the ground without your Father's knowledge. Even all the hairs of your head are counted. So do not be afraid; you are worth more than many sparrows. Everyone who acknowledges me before others I will acknowledge before my heavenly Father. But whoever denies me before others, I will deny before my heavenly Father."

Meditation (*Meditatio*)

After the reading, take some time to reflect in silence on one or more of the following questions:

- What word or words in this passage caught your attention?
- What in this passage comforted you?
- What in this passage challenged you?

If practicing lectio divina as a family or in a group, after the reflection time, invite the participants to share their responses.

Prayer (*Oratio*)

Read the scripture passage one more time. Bring to the Lord the praise, petition, or thanksgiving that the Word inspires in you.

Contemplation (*Contemplatio*)

Read the Scripture again, followed by this reflection:

≈ What conversion of mind, heart, and life is the Lord asking of me?

_____

_____

_____

_____

≈ *Fear no one.* What do I fear? How do my fears inhibit my following God's will for me?

_____

_____

_____

_____

~ *You are worth more than many sparrows.* How do I show that my life is a gift from God? How do I demonstrate respect for my dignity and that of others?

_____

_____

_____

_____

~ *Everyone who acknowledges me before others I will acknowledge before my heavenly Father.* How have I given witness to my faith in God? How does my way of living reflect what I believe?

_____

_____

_____

_____

~ *After a period of silent reflection and/or discussion, all recite the Lord's Prayer and the following:*

Closing Prayer

For your sake I bear insult,
    and shame covers my face.
I have become an outcast to my brothers,
    a stranger to my mother's children,
Because zeal for your house consumes me,
    and the insults of those who blaspheme you fall upon me.

I pray to you, O LORD,
    for the time of your favor, O God!
In your great kindness answer me
    with your constant help.
Answer me, O LORD, for bounteous is your kindness;
    in your great mercy turn toward me.

"See, you lowly ones, and be glad;
    you who seek God, may your hearts revive!
For the LORD hears the poor,
    and his own who are in bonds he spurns not.
Let the heavens and the earth praise him,
    the seas and whatever moves in them!"

From Psalm 69

Living the Word This Week

How can I make my life a gift for others in charity?

Share your faith by taking some action that supports the dignity of all human beings: write to a legislator, feed the homeless, support women in crisis pregnancies, etc.

July 2, 2023

Lectio Divina for the Thirteenth Week in Ordinary Time

We begin our prayer:

In the name of the Father, and of the Son, and of the Holy Spirit. Amen.

O God, who through the grace of adoption
chose us to be children of light,
grant, we pray,
that we may not be wrapped in the darkness of error
but always be seen to stand in the bright light of truth.
Through our Lord Jesus Christ, your Son,
who lives and reigns with you in the unity of the Holy Spirit,
God, for ever and ever.

Collect, Thirteenth Sunday in Ordinary Time

Reading (*Lectio*)

Read the following Scripture two or three times.

Matthew 10:37-42

> Jesus said to his apostles: "Whoever loves father or mother more than me is not worthy of me, and whoever loves son or daughter more than me is not worthy of me; and whoever does not take up his cross and follow after me is not worthy of me. Whoever finds his life will lose it, and whoever loses his life for my sake will find it.

> "Whoever receives you receives me, and whoever receives me receives the one who sent me. Whoever receives a prophet because he is a prophet will receive a prophet's reward, and whoever receives a righteous man because he is a righteous man will receive a righteous man's reward. And whoever gives only a cup of cold water to one of these little ones to drink because the little one is a disciple—amen, I say to you, he will surely not lose his reward."

Meditation (*Meditatio*)

After the reading, take some time to reflect in silence on one or more of the following questions:

- What word or words in this passage caught your attention?
- What in this passage comforted you?
- What in this passage challenged you?

If practicing lectio divina *as a family or in a group, after the reflection time, invite the participants to share their responses.*

Prayer (*Oratio*)

Read the scripture passage one more time. Bring to the Lord the praise, petition, or thanksgiving that the Word inspires in you.

Contemplation (*Contemplatio*)

Read the Scripture again, followed by this reflection:

≈ What conversion of mind, heart, and life is the Lord asking of me?

_____

_____

_____

_____

≈ *Whoever loves father or mother more than me is not worthy of me.* What do I love more than God? How can I re-orient my life to place God at its center?

_____

_____

_____

_____

~ *Whoever does not take up his cross and follow after me is not worthy of me.* What cross is Jesus asking me to carry this week? Is there someone I can help to carry his or her cross?

_____

_____

_____

_____

~ *Whoever receives you receives me, and whoever receives me receives the one who sent me.* Who is excluded from my welcome? How can I be more welcoming?

_____

_____

_____

_____

~ *After a period of silent reflection and/or discussion, all recite the Lord's Prayer and the following:*

Closing Prayer

The promises of the LORD I will sing forever,
    through all generations my mouth shall proclaim your
    faithfulness.
For you have said, "My kindness is established forever;"

in heaven you have confirmed your faithfulness.

Blessed the people who know the joyful shout;
    in the light of your countenance, O LORD, they walk.
At your name they rejoice all the day,
    and through your justice they are exalted.

You are the splendor of their strength,
    and by your favor our horn is exalted.
For to the LORD belongs our shield,
    and the Holy One of Israel, our king.

From Psalm 89

Living the Word This Week

How can I make my life a gift for others in charity?

Read and reflect on *Strangers No Longer*: www.usccb.org/
issues-and-action/human-life-and-dignity/immigration/
strangers-no-longer-together-on-the-journey-of-hope

July 9, 2023

Lectio Divina for the Fourteenth Week in Ordinary Time

We begin our prayer:

In the name of the Father, and of the Son, and of the Holy Spirit. Amen.

O God, who in the abasement of your Son
have raised up a fallen world,
fill your faithful with holy joy,
for on those you have rescued from slavery to sin
you bestow eternal gladness.
Through our Lord Jesus Christ, your Son,
who lives and reigns with you in the unity of the Holy Spirit,
God, for ever and ever.

Collect, Fourteenth Sunday in Ordinary Time

Reading (*Lectio*)

Read the following Scripture two or three times.

Matthew 11:25-30

> At that time Jesus exclaimed: "I give praise to you, Father, Lord of heaven and earth, for although you have hidden these things from the wise and the learned you have revealed them to little ones. Yes, Father, such has been your gracious will. All things have been handed over to me by my Father. No one knows the Son except the Father, and no one knows the Father except the Son and anyone to whom the Son wishes to reveal him."

> "Come to me, all you who labor and are burdened, and I will give you rest. Take my yoke upon you and learn from me, for I am meek and humble of heart; and you will find rest for yourselves. For my yoke is easy, and my burden light."

Meditation (*Meditatio*)

After the reading, take some time to reflect in silence on one or more of the following questions:

- What word or words in this passage caught your attention?
- What in this passage comforted you?
- What in this passage challenged you?

If practicing lectio divina *as a family or in a group, after the reflection time, invite the participants to share their responses.*

Prayer (*Oratio*)

Read the scripture passage one more time. Bring to the Lord the praise, petition, or thanksgiving that the Word inspires in you.

Contemplation (*Contemplatio*)

Read the Scripture again, followed by this reflection:

~ What conversion of mind, heart, and life is the Lord asking of me?

_____

_____

_____

_____

~ *Yes, Father, such has been your gracious will.* How can I better discern God's will for my life? How can I become more docile to God's will and the promptings of the Holy Spirit?

_____

_____

_____

_____

≈ *No one knows the Son except the Father, and no one knows the Father except the Son and anyone to whom the Son wishes to reveal him.* How do I come to know God better? How can I help others know God?

_____

_____

_____

_____

≈ *I am meek and humble of heart.* How can I grow in humility? How can I place others' needs before my own?

_____

_____

_____

_____

≈ *After a period of silent reflection and/or discussion, all recite the Lord's Prayer and the following:*

Closing Prayer

I will extol you, O my God and King,
and I will bless your name forever and ever.
Every day will I bless you,
and I will praise your name forever and ever.

The Lord is gracious and merciful,
   slow to anger and of great kindness.
The Lord is good to all
   and compassionate toward all his works.

Let all your works give you thanks, O Lord,
   and let your faithful ones bless you.
Let them discourse of the glory of your kingdom
   and speak of your might.

The Lord is faithful in all his words
   and holy in all his works.
The Lord lifts up all who are falling
   and raises up all who are bowed down.

From Psalm 145

Living the Word This Week

How can I make my life a gift for others in charity?

Consider contributing your time, treasure, or talent to a local agency
that aids the poor, such as the Saint Vincent de Paul Society or
Catholic Charities.

July 16, 2023

Lectio Divina for the Fifteenth Week in Ordinary Time

We begin our prayer:

In the name of the Father, and of the Son, and of the Holy Spirit. Amen.

O God, who show the light of your truth
to those who go astray,
so that they may return to the right path,
give all who for the faith they profess
are accounted Christians
the grace to reject whatever is contrary to the name of Christ
and to strive after all that does it honor.
Through our Lord Jesus Christ, your Son,
who lives and reigns with you in the unity of the Holy Spirit,
God, for ever and ever.

Collect, Fifteenth Sunday in Ordinary Time

Reading (*Lectio*)

Read the following Scripture two or three times.

Matthew 13:1-23

On that day, Jesus went out of the house and sat down by the sea. Such large crowds gathered around him that he got into a boat and sat down, and the whole crowd stood along the shore.

And he spoke to them at length in parables, saying: "A sower went out to sow. And as he sowed, some seed fell on the path, and birds came and ate it up. Some fell on rocky ground, where it had little soil. It sprang up at once because the soil was not deep, and when the sun rose it was scorched, and it withered for lack of roots. Some seed fell among thorns, and the thorns grew up and choked it. But some seed fell on rich soil, and produced fruit, a hundred or sixty or thirtyfold. Whoever has ears ought to hear."

The disciples approached him and said, "Why do you speak to them in parables?" He said to them in reply, "Because knowledge of the mysteries of the kingdom of heaven has been granted to you, but to them it has not been granted. To anyone who has, more will be given and he will grow rich; from anyone who has not, even what he has will be taken away. This is why I speak to them in parables, because *they look but do not see and hear but do not listen or understand.*

Isaiah's prophecy is fulfilled in them, which says:

You shall indeed hear but not understand,
*   you shall indeed look but never see.*
Gross is the heart of this people,
*   they will hardly hear with their ears,*
*   they have closed their eyes,*
*   lest they see with their eyes*
*   and hear with their ears*
and understand with their hearts and be converted,
*   and I heal them.*

"But blessed are your eyes, because they see, and your ears, because they hear. Amen, I say to you, many prophets and righteous people longed to see what you see but did not see it, and to hear what you hear but did not hear it.

"Hear then the parable of the sower. The seed sown on the path is the one who hears the word of the kingdom without understanding it, and the evil one comes and steals away what was sown in his heart. The seed sown on rocky ground is the one who hears the word and receives it at once with joy. But he has no root and lasts only for a time. When some tribulation or persecution comes because of the word, he immediately falls away. The seed sown among thorns is the one who hears the word, but then worldly anxiety and the lure of riches choke the word and it bears no fruit. But the seed sown on rich soil is the one who hears the word and understands it, who indeed bears fruit and yields a hundred or sixty or thirtyfold."

Meditation (*Meditatio*)

After the reading, take some time to reflect in silence on one or more of the following questions:

- What word or words in this passage caught your attention?
- What in this passage comforted you?
- What in this passage challenged you?

If practicing lectio divina *as a family or in a group, after the reflection time, invite the participants to share their responses.*

Prayer (*Oratio*)

Read the scripture passage one more time. Bring to the Lord the praise, petition, or thanksgiving that the Word inspires in you.

Contemplation (*Contemplatio*)

Read the Scripture again, followed by this reflection:

≈ What conversion of mind, heart, and life is the Lord asking of me?

_____

_____

_____

_____

≈ *And he spoke to them at length in parables.* How does God speak to me? How can I become more attentive to God's voice?

_____

_____

_____

_____

≈ *Because knowledge of the mysteries of the kingdom of heaven has been granted to you.* How do I learn about my faith and the mysteries of the kingdom of heaven? Who has shared this knowledge with me?

_____

_____

_____

_____

≈ *When some tribulation or persecution comes because of the word, he immediately falls away.* What distracts me from my faith and God's Word? How can I grow in steadfastness and hope?

_____

_____

_____

_____

~ After a period of silent reflection and/or discussion, all recite the Lord's Prayer and the following:

Closing Prayer

You have visited the land and watered it;
>   greatly have you enriched it.
God's watercourses are filled;
>   you have prepared the grain.

Thus have you prepared the land: drenching its furrows,
>   breaking up its clods,
Softening it with showers,
>   blessing its yield.

You have crowned the year with your bounty,
>   and your paths overflow with a rich harvest;
The untilled meadows overflow with it,
>   and rejoicing clothes the hills.

The fields are garmented with flocks
>   and the valleys blanketed with grain.
>   They shout and sing for joy.

From Psalm 65

Living the Word This Week

How can I make my life a gift for others in charity?

Consider volunteering as a catechist for children or adults.

July 23, 2023

Lectio Divina for the Sixteenth Week in Ordinary Time

We begin our prayer:

In the name of the Father, and of the Son, and of the Holy Spirit. Amen.

Show favor, O Lord, to your servants
and mercifully increase the gifts of your grace,
that, made fervent in hope, faith and charity,
they may be ever watchful in keeping your commands.
Through our Lord Jesus Christ, your Son,
who lives and reigns with you in the unity of the Holy Spirit,
God, for ever and ever.

Collect, Sixteenth Sunday in Ordinary Time

Reading (*Lectio*)

Read the following Scripture two or three times.

Matthew 13:24-43

Jesus proposed another parable to the crowds, saying: "The kingdom of heaven may be likened to a man who sowed good seed in his field. While everyone was asleep his enemy came and sowed weeds all through the wheat, and then went off. When the crop grew and bore fruit, the weeds appeared as well. The slaves of the householder came to him and said, 'Master, did you not sow good seed in your field? Where have the weeds come from?' He answered, 'An enemy has done this.' His slaves said to him, 'Do you want us to go and pull them up?' He replied, 'No, if you pull up the weeds you might uproot the wheat along with them. Let them grow together until harvest; then at harvest time I will say to the harvesters, "First collect the weeds and tie them in bundles for burning; but gather the wheat into my barn."'"

He proposed another parable to them. "The kingdom of heaven is like a mustard seed that a person took and sowed in a field. It is the smallest of all the seeds, yet when full-grown it is the largest of plants. It becomes a large bush, and the 'birds of the sky come and dwell in its branches.'"

He spoke to them another parable. "The kingdom of heaven is like yeast that a woman took and mixed with three measures of wheat flour until the whole batch was leavened."

All these things Jesus spoke to the crowds in parables. He spoke to them only in parables, to fulfill what had been said through the prophet:

I will open my mouth in parables,
I will announce what has lain hidden from the foundation of the world.

Then, dismissing the crowds, he went into the house. His disciples approached him and said, "Explain to us the parable of the weeds in the field." He said in reply, "He who sows good seed is the Son of Man, the field is the world, the good seed the children of the kingdom. The weeds are the children of the evil one, and the enemy who sows them is the devil. The harvest is the end of the age, and the harvesters are angels. Just as weeds are collected and burned up with fire, so will it be at the end of the age. The Son of Man will send his angels, and they will collect out of his kingdom all who cause others to sin and all evildoers. They will throw them into the fiery furnace, where there will be wailing and grinding of teeth. Then the righteous will shine like the sun in the kingdom of their Father. Whoever has ears ought to hear."

Meditation (*Meditatio*)

After the reading, take some time to reflect in silence on one or more of the following questions:

- What word or words in this passage caught your attention?
- What in this passage comforted you?
- What in this passage challenged you?

If practicing lectio divina *as a family or in a group, after the reflection time, invite the participants to share their responses.*

Prayer (*Oratio*)

Read the scripture passage one more time. Bring to the Lord the praise, petition, or thanksgiving that the Word inspires in you.

Contemplation (*Contemplatio*)

Read the Scripture again, followed by this reflection:

~ What conversion of mind, heart, and life is the Lord asking of me?

_____

_____

_____

_____

~ *When the crop grew and bore fruit, the weeds appeared as well.* What fruit does faith bear in my life? What weeds keep my life from being more fruitful?

_____

_____

_____

_____

~ *The field is the world.* Where is the field that God is calling me to work in? What labor can I give to help those around me?

_____

_____

_____

_____

~ *Then the righteous will shine like the sun in the kingdom of their Father.* How can I glorify the Lord by life? How can I better share my faith?

_____

_____

_____

_____

~ *After a period of silent reflection and/or discussion, all recite the Lord's Prayer and the following:*

Closing Prayer

You, O LORD, are good and forgiving,
  abounding in kindness to all who call upon you.
Hearken, O LORD, to my prayer
  and attend to the sound of my pleading.

All the nations you have made shall come
    and worship you, O Lord,
    and glorify your name.
For you are great, and you do wondrous deeds;
    you alone are God.

You, O Lord, are a God merciful and gracious,
    slow to anger, abounding in kindness and fidelity.
Turn toward me, and have pity on me;
    give your strength to your servant.

From Psalm 86

Living the Word This Week

How can I make my life a gift for others in charity?

Make a good examination of conscience and receive the Sacrament of Penance.

July 30, 2023

Lectio Divina for the Seventeenth Week in Ordinary Time

We begin our prayer:

In the name of the Father, and of the Son, and of the Holy Spirit. Amen.

O God, protector of those who hope in you,
without whom nothing has firm foundation, nothing is holy,
bestow in abundance your mercy upon us
and grant that, with you as our ruler and guide,
we may use the good things that pass
in such a way as to hold fast even now
to those that ever endure.
Through our Lord Jesus Christ, your Son,
who lives and reigns with you in the unity of the Holy Spirit,
God, for ever and ever.

Collect, Seventeenth Sunday in Ordinary Time

Reading (*Lectio*)

Read the following Scripture two or three times.

Matthew 13:44-52

Jesus said to his disciples: "The kingdom of heaven is like a treasure buried in a field, which a person finds and hides again, and out of joy goes and sells all that he has and buys that field. Again, the kingdom of heaven is like a merchant searching for fine pearls. When he finds a pearl of great price, he goes and sells all that he has and buys it. Again, the kingdom of heaven is like a net thrown into the sea, which collects fish of every kind. When it is full they haul it ashore and sit down to put what is good into buckets. What is bad they throw away. Thus it will be at the end of the age. The angels will go out and separate the wicked from the righteous and throw them into the fiery furnace, where there will be wailing and grinding of teeth.

"Do you understand all these things?" They answered, "Yes." And he replied, "Then every scribe who has been instructed in the kingdom of heaven is like the head of a household who brings from his storeroom both the new and the old."

Meditation (*Meditatio*)

After the reading, take some time to reflect in silence on one or more of the following questions:

- What word or words in this passage caught your attention?
- What in this passage comforted you?
- What in this passage challenged you?

If practicing lectio divina *as a family or in a group, after the reflection time, invite the participants to share their responses.*

Prayer (*Oratio*)

Read the scripture passage one more time. Bring to the Lord the praise, petition, or thanksgiving that the Word inspires in you.

Contemplation (*Contemplatio*)

Read the Scripture again, followed by this reflection:

What conversion of mind, heart, and life is the Lord asking of me?

Again, the kingdom of heaven is like a merchant searching for fine pearls. What am I searching for? How do I decide what is truly of value?

Again, the kingdom of heaven is like a net thrown into the sea, which collects fish of every kind. How do I treat those who are different from me? How can I learn to see Jesus in everyone I meet?

Then every scribe who has been instructed in the kingdom of heaven is like the head of a household who brings from his storeroom both the new and the old. How do I show respect for tradition and the things of the past? How do I remain open to what the Holy Spirit is doing in the Church and in the world?

After a period of silent reflection and/or discussion, all recite the Lord's Prayer and the following:

Closing Prayer

I have said, O LORD, that my part
  is to keep your words.
The law of your mouth is to me more precious
  than thousands of gold and silver pieces.

Let your kindness comfort me
  according to your promise to your servants.
Let your compassion come to me that I may live,
  for your law is my delight.

For I love your command
  more than gold, however fine.
For in all your precepts I go forward;
  every false way I hate.

Wonderful are your decrees;
  therefore I observe them.
The revelation of your words sheds light,
  giving understanding to the simple.

From Psalm 119

Living the Word This Week

How can I make my life a gift for others in charity?

Commit to some time for spiritual reading (the Bible, the lives of the Saints, the Catechism, papal documents, etc.) each day for the next month.

August 6, 2023

Lectio Divina for the Feast of the Transfiguration of the Lord

We begin our prayer:

In the name of the Father, and of the Son, and of the Holy Spirit. Amen.

O God, who in the glorious Transfiguration
of your Only Begotten Son
confirmed the mysteries of faith by the witness of the Fathers
and wonderfully prefigured our full adoption to sonship,
grant, we pray, to your servants,
that, listening to the voice of your beloved Son,
we may merit to become co-heirs with him.
Who lives and reigns with you in the unity of the Holy Spirit,
God, for ever and ever.

Collect, Feast of the Transfiguration of the Lord

Reading (*Lectio*)

Read the following Scripture two or three times.

Matthew 17:1-9

> Jesus took Peter, James, and his brother, John, and led them up a high mountain by themselves. And he was transfigured before them; his face shone like the sun and his clothes became white as light. And behold, Moses and Elijah appeared to them, conversing with him. Then Peter said to Jesus in reply, "Lord, it is good that we are here. If you wish, I will make three tents here, one for you, one for Moses, and one for Elijah." While he was still speaking, behold, a bright cloud cast a shadow over them, then from the cloud came a voice that said, "This is my beloved Son, with whom I am well pleased; listen to him." When the disciples heard this, they fell prostrate and were very much afraid. But Jesus came and touched them, saying, "Rise, and do not be afraid." And when the disciples raised their eyes, they saw no one else but Jesus alone.

> As they were coming down from the mountain, Jesus charged them, "Do not tell the vision to anyone until the Son of Man has been raised from the dead."

Meditation (*Meditatio*)

After the reading, take some time to reflect in silence on one or more of the following questions:

- What word or words in this passage caught your attention?
- What in this passage comforted you?
- What in this passage challenged you?

If practicing lectio divina *as a family or in a group, after the reflection time, invite the participants to share their responses.*

Prayer (*Oratio*)

Read the scripture passage one more time. Bring to the Lord the praise, petition, or thanksgiving that the Word inspires in you.

Contemplation (*Contemplatio*)

Read the Scripture again, followed by this reflection:

∾ What conversion of mind, heart, and life is the Lord asking of me?

_____

_____

_____

_____

∾ *Jesus took Peter, James, and his brother, John, and led them up a high mountain by themselves.* Where can I go to be alone with God? In what places do I like to pray?

_____

_____

_____

_____

≈ *Lord, it is good that we are here.* Who has accompanied me through the difficult times in my life? How can I accompany my brothers and sisters who are struggling?

_____

_____

_____

_____

≈ *And when the disciples raised their eyes, they saw no one else but Jesus alone.* What distracts me from following Jesus? How can I keep my sights on Jesus?

_____

_____

_____

_____

≈ *After a period of silent reflection and/or discussion, all recite the Lord's Prayer and the following:*

Closing Prayer

The LORD is king; let the earth rejoice;
    let the many islands be glad.
Clouds and darkness are round about him,
    justice and judgment are the foundation of his throne.

The mountains melt like wax before the Lord,
    before the Lord of all the earth.
The heavens proclaim his justice,
    and all peoples see his glory.

Because you, O Lord, are the Most High over all the earth,
    exalted far above all gods.

From Psalm 97

Living the Word This Week

How can I make my life a gift for others in charity?

Read and reflect on the appeal in paragraph 285 of
Pope Francis' encyclical *Fratelli tutti*: https://www.
vatican.va/content/francesco/en/encyclicals/documents/
papa-francesco_20201003_enciclica-fratelli-tutti.html

August 13, 2023

Lectio Divina for the Nineteenth Week in Ordinary Time

We begin our prayer:

In the name of the Father, and of the Son, and of the Holy Spirit. Amen.

Almighty ever-living God,
whom, taught by the Holy Spirit,
we dare to call our Father,
bring, we pray, to perfection in our hearts
the spirit of adoption as your sons and daughters,
that we may merit to enter into the inheritance
which you have promised.
Through our Lord Jesus Christ, your Son,
who lives and reigns with you in the unity of the Holy Spirit,
God, for ever and ever.

Collect, Nineteenth Sunday in Ordinary Time

Reading (*Lectio*)

Read the following Scripture two or three times.

Matthew 14:22-33

> After he had fed the people, Jesus made the disciples get into a boat and precede him to the other side, while he dismissed the crowds. After doing so, he went up on the mountain by himself to pray. When it was evening he was there alone. Meanwhile the boat, already a few miles offshore, was being tossed about by the waves, for the wind was against it. During the fourth watch of the night, he came toward them walking on the sea. When the disciples saw him walking on the sea they were terrified. "It is a ghost," they said, and they cried out in fear. At once Jesus spoke to them, "Take courage, it is I; do not be afraid." Peter said to him in reply, "Lord, if it is you, command me to come to you on the water." He said, "Come." Peter got out of the boat and began to walk on the water toward Jesus. But when he saw how strong the wind was he became frightened; and, beginning to sink, he cried out, "Lord, save me!" Immediately Jesus stretched out his hand and caught Peter, and said to him, "O you of little faith, why did you doubt?" After they got into the boat, the wind died down. Those who were in the boat did him homage, saying, "Truly, you are the Son of God."

Meditation (*Meditatio*)

After the reading, take some time to reflect in silence on one or more of the following questions:

- What word or words in this passage caught your attention?
- What in this passage comforted you?
- What in this passage challenged you?

If practicing lectio divina *as a family or in a group, after the reflection time, invite the participants to share their responses.*

Prayer (*Oratio*)

Read the scripture passage one more time. Bring to the Lord the praise, petition, or thanksgiving that the Word inspires in you.

Contemplation (*Contemplatio*)

Read the Scripture again, followed by this reflection:

≈ What conversion of mind, heart, and life is the Lord asking of me?

_____

_____

_____

_____

≈ *When it was evening he was there alone.* When have I felt most alone? How can I be present to those who have no one?

_____

_____

_____

_____

≈ *During the fourth watch of the night, he came toward them walking on the sea.* When have I seen the power of God displayed? How can I grow in trust of God's awesome power?

_____

_____

_____

_____

≈ *Lord, if it is you, command me to come to you on the water.* When have I been tempted to test the Lord? When has my faith been plagued by doubts?

_____

_____

_____

_____

≈ *After a period of silent reflection and/or discussion, all recite the Lord's Prayer and the following:*

Closing Prayer

I will hear what God proclaims;
    the LORD — for he proclaims peace.
Near indeed is his salvation to those who fear him,
    glory dwelling in our land.

Kindness and truth shall meet;
    justice and peace shall kiss.
Truth shall spring out of the earth,
    and justice shall look down from heaven.

The LORD himself will give his benefits;
    our land shall yield its increase.
Justice shall walk before him,
    and prepare the way of his steps.

From Psalm 85

Living the Word This Week

How can I make my life a gift for others in charity?

Reach out to someone who is homebound, incarcerated, unhoused, or otherwise alone.

August 15, 2023

Lectio Divina for the Solemnity of the Assumption of the Blessed Virgin Mary

We begin our prayer:

In the name of the Father, and of the Son, and of the Holy Spirit. Amen.

Almighty ever-living God,
who assumed the Immaculate Virgin Mary, the Mother of your Son,
body and soul into heavenly glory,
grant, we pray,
that, always attentive to the things that are above,
we may merit to be sharers of her glory.
Through our Lord Jesus Christ, your Son,
who lives and reigns with you in the unity of the Holy Spirit,
God, for ever and ever.

Collect, Solemnity of the Assumption, Mass During the Day

Reading (*Lectio*)

Read the following Scripture two or three times.

Luke 1:39-56

Mary set out and traveled to the hill country in haste to a town of Judah, where she entered the house of Zechariah and greeted Elizabeth. When Elizabeth heard Mary's greeting, the infant leaped in her womb, and Elizabeth, filled with the Holy Spirit, cried out in a loud voice and said, "Blessed are you among women, and blessed is the fruit of your womb. And how does this happen to me, that the mother of my Lord should come to me? For at the moment the sound of your greeting reached my ears, the infant in my womb leaped for joy. Blessed are you who believed that what was spoken to you by the Lord would be fulfilled."

And Mary said:

"My soul proclaims the greatness of the Lord;
    my spirit rejoices in God my Savior
    for he has looked with favor on his lowly servant.
From this day all generations will call me blessed:
    the Almighty has done great things for me
    and holy is his Name.
    He has mercy on those who fear him
    in every generation.
He has shown the strength of his arm,
    and has scattered the proud in their conceit.
He has cast down the mighty from their thrones,
    and has lifted up the lowly.
He has filled the hungry with good things,
    and the rich he has sent away empty.

He has come to the help of his servant Israel
for he has remembered his promise of mercy,
the promise he made to our fathers,
to Abraham and his children forever."

Mary remained with her about three months and then returned to her home.

Meditation (*Meditatio*)

After the reading, take some time to reflect in silence on one or more of the following questions:

- What word or words in this passage caught your attention?
- What in this passage comforted you?
- What in this passage challenged you?

If practicing lectio divina *as a family or in a group, after the reflection time, invite the participants to share their responses.*

Prayer (*Oratio*)

Read the scripture passage one more time. Bring to the Lord the praise, petition, or thanksgiving that the Word inspires in you.

Contemplation (*Contemplatio*)

Read the Scripture again, followed by this reflection:

≈ What conversion of mind, heart, and life is the Lord asking of me?

_____

_____

_____

_____

≈ *Elizabeth, filled with the Holy Spirit, cried out in a loud voice.* How do I experience the presence of the Holy Spirit in my life? How do I share the Spirit's gifts with those around me?

_____

_____

_____

_____

≈ *From this day all generations will call me blessed:/the Almighty has done great things for me.* How has God blessed me today? For what blessings and I most thankful?

_____

_____

~ *He has filled the hungry with good things,/and the rich he has sent away empty.* How attentive am I to the needs of others? What can I change about my own habits so that I can share more generously?

_____

_____

_____

_____

~ *After a period of silent reflection and/or discussion, all recite the Lord's Prayer and the following:*

Closing Prayer

The queen takes her place at your right hand in gold of Ophir.

Hear, O daughter, and see; turn your ear,
    forget your people and your father's house.

So shall the king desire your beauty;
    for he is your lord.

They are borne in with gladness and joy;
    they enter the palace of the king.

From Psalm 45

Living the Word This Week

How can I make my life a gift for others in charity?

Pray the Rosary for the intentions of the Holy Father.

August 20, 2023

Lectio Divina for the Twentieth Week in Ordinary Time

We begin our prayer:

In the name of the Father, and of the Son, and of the Holy Spirit. Amen.

O God, who have prepared for those who love you
good things which no eye can see,
fill our hearts, we pray, with the warmth of your love,
so that, loving you in all things and above all things,
we may attain your promises,
which surpass every human desire.
Through our Lord Jesus Christ, your Son,
who lives and reigns with you in the unity of the Holy Spirit,
God, for ever and ever.

Collect, Twentieth Sunday in Ordinary Time

Reading (*Lectio*)

Read the following Scripture two or three times.

Matthew 15:21-28

> At that time, Jesus withdrew to the region of Tyre and Sidon. And behold, a Canaanite woman of that district came and called out, "Have pity on me, Lord, Son of David! My daughter is tormented by a demon." But Jesus did not say a word in answer to her. Jesus' disciples came and asked him, "Send her away, for she keeps calling out after us." He said in reply, "I was sent only to the lost sheep of the house of Israel." But the woman came and did Jesus homage, saying, "Lord, help me." He said in reply, "It is not right to take the food of the children and throw it to the dogs." She said, "Please, Lord, for even the dogs eat the scraps that fall from the table of their masters." Then Jesus said to her in reply, "O woman, great is your faith! Let it be done for you as you wish." And the woman's daughter was healed from that hour.

Meditation (*Meditatio*)

After the reading, take some time to reflect in silence on one or more of the following questions:

- What word or words in this passage caught your attention?
- What in this passage comforted you?
- What in this passage challenged you?

If practicing lectio divina *as a family or in a group, after the reflection time, invite the participants to share their responses.*

Prayer (*Oratio*)

Read the scripture passage one more time. Bring to the Lord the praise, petition, or thanksgiving that the Word inspires in you.

Contemplation (*Contemplatio*)

Read the Scripture again, followed by this reflection:

∾ What conversion of mind, heart, and life is the Lord asking of me?

_____

_____

_____

_____

∾ *Have pity on me, Lord, Son of David!* What struggles do I need to bring to the Lord? Who needs my assistance?

_____

_____

_____

_____

~ *Send her away, for she keeps calling out after us.* Who do I tend to judge or exclude? How can I be more welcoming to those who are different from me?

_____

_____

_____

_____

~ *Let it be done for you as you wish.* How has God answered my prayers in the past? For what do I need to ask the Lord today?

_____

_____

_____

_____

~ *After a period of silent reflection and/or discussion, all recite the Lord's Prayer and the following:*

Closing Prayer

May God have pity on us and bless us;
    may he let his face shine upon us.
So may your way be known upon earth;
    among all nations, your salvation.

May the nations be glad and exult
  because you rule the peoples in equity;
  the nations on the earth you guide.

May the peoples praise you, O God;
  may all the peoples praise you!
May God bless us,
  and may all the ends of the earth fear him!

From Psalm 67

Living the Word This Week

How can I make my life a gift for others in charity?

Read and reflect on *Open Wide our Hearts: An Enduring Call to Love*:
https://www.usccb.org/issues-and-action/human-life-and-dignity/
racism/upload/open-wide-our-hearts.pdf

August 27, 2023

Lectio Divina for the Twenty-First Week in Ordinary Time

We begin our prayer:

In the name of the Father, and of the Son, and of the Holy Spirit. Amen.

O God, who cause the minds of the faithful
to unite in a single purpose,
grant your people to love what you command
and to desire what you promise,
that, amid the uncertainties of this world,
our hearts may be fixed on that place
where true gladness is found.
Through our Lord Jesus Christ, your Son,
who lives and reigns with you in the unity of the Holy Spirit,
God, for ever and ever.

Collect, Twenty-First Sunday in Ordinary Time

Reading (*Lectio*)

Read the following Scripture two or three times.

Matthew 16:13-20

> Jesus went into the region of Caesarea Philippi and he asked his disciples, "Who do people say that the Son of Man is?" They replied, "Some say John the Baptist, others Elijah, still others Jeremiah or one of the prophets." He said to them, "But who do you say that I am?" Simon Peter said in reply, "You are the Christ, the Son of the living God." Jesus said to him in reply, "Blessed are you, Simon son of Jonah. For flesh and blood has not revealed this to you, but my heavenly Father. And so I say to you, you are Peter, and upon this rock I will build my church, and the gates of the netherworld shall not prevail against it. I will give you the keys to the kingdom of heaven. Whatever you bind on earth shall be bound in heaven; and whatever you loose on earth shall be loosed in heaven." Then he strictly ordered his disciples to tell no one that he was the Christ.

Meditation (*Meditatio*)

After the reading, take some time to reflect in silence on one or more of the following questions:

- What word or words in this passage caught your attention?
- What in this passage comforted you?
- What in this passage challenged you?

If practicing lectio divina *as a family or in a group, after the reflection time, invite the participants to share their responses.*

Prayer (*Oratio*)

Read the scripture passage one more time. Bring to the Lord the praise, petition, or thanksgiving that the Word inspires in you.

Contemplation (*Contemplatio*)

Read the Scripture again, followed by this reflection:

≈ What conversion of mind, heart, and life is the Lord asking of me?

_____

_____

_____

_____

≈ *You are the Christ, the Son of the living God.* How do I encounter the living God in my daily life? How can I live so as to share eternal life in heaven?

_____

_____

_____

_____

~ *The gates of the netherworld shall not prevail against it.* Where do I see evil present in the world? How can I resist the lure of evil?

_____

_____

_____

_____

~ *Whatever you bind on earth shall be bound in heaven; and whatever you loose on earth shall be loosed in heaven.* What sinful behaviors should I work to avoid? What virtues should I seek to foster?

_____

_____

_____

_____

~ *After a period of silent reflection and/or discussion, all recite the Lord's Prayer and the following:*

Closing Prayer

I will give thanks to you, O Lord, with all my heart,
for you have heard the words of my mouth;
in the presence of the angels I will sing your praise;
I will worship at your holy temple.

I will give thanks to your name,
   because of your kindness and your truth:
When I called, you answered me;
   you built up strength within me.

The LORD is exalted, yet the lowly he sees,
   and the proud he knows from afar.
Your kindness, O LORD, endures forever;
   forsake not the work of your hands.

From Psalm 138

Living the Word This Week

How can I make my life a gift for others in charity?

Read about the foundations of the Christian moral life by reading Chapter 23 of the *United States Catholic Catechism for Adults:* https://www.usccb.org/sites/default/files/flipbooks/uscca/files/assets/basic-html/page-335.html

September 3, 2023

Lectio Divina for the Twenty-Second Week in Ordinary Time

We begin our prayer:

In the name of the Father, and of the Son, and of the Holy Spirit. Amen.

God of might, giver of every good gift,
put into our hearts the love of your name,
so that, by deepening our sense of reverence,
you may nurture in us what is good
and, by your watchful care,
keep safe what you have nurtured.
Through our Lord Jesus Christ, your Son,
who lives and reigns with you in the unity of the Holy Spirit,
God, for ever and ever.

Collect, Twenty-Second Sunday in Ordinary Time

Reading (*Lectio*)

Read the following Scripture two or three times.

Matthew 16:21-27

> Jesus began to show his disciples that he must go to Jerusalem and suffer greatly from the elders, the chief priests, and the scribes, and be killed and on the third day be raised. Then Peter took Jesus aside and began to rebuke him, "God forbid, Lord! No such thing shall ever happen to you." He turned and said to Peter, "Get behind me, Satan! You are an obstacle to me. You are thinking not as God does, but as human beings do."
>
> Then Jesus said to his disciples, "Whoever wishes to come after me must deny himself, take up his cross, and follow me. For whoever wishes to save his life will lose it, but whoever loses his life for my sake will find it. What profit would there be for one to gain the whole world and forfeit his life? Or what can one give in exchange for his life? For the Son of Man will come with his angels in his Father's glory, and then he will repay all according to his conduct."

Meditation (*Meditatio*)

After the reading, take some time to reflect in silence on one or more of the following questions:

- What word or words in this passage caught your attention?
- What in this passage comforted you?
- What in this passage challenged you?

If practicing lectio divina *as a family or in a group, after the reflection time, invite the participants to share their responses.*

Prayer (*Oratio*)

Read the scripture passage one more time. Bring to the Lord the praise, petition, or thanksgiving that the Word inspires in you.

Contemplation (*Contemplatio*)

Read the Scripture again, followed by this reflection:

≈ What conversion of mind, heart, and life is the Lord asking of me?

_____

_____

_____

_____

≈ *You are an obstacle to me.* What people, places, or things are obstacles to my growth in faith? How have I been an obstacle to others' faith?

_____

_____

_____

_____

~ *You are thinking not as God does, but as human beings do.* When have I judged my circumstances with the world's values? When have I judged my circumstances in accord with God's will?

_____

_____

_____

_____

~ *Whoever wishes to come after me must deny himself, take up his cross, and follow me.* What cross do I need to bear? How can I give of myself to help others bear their crosses?

_____

_____

_____

_____

~ *After a period of silent reflection and/or discussion, all recite the Lord's Prayer and the following:*

Closing Prayer

O God, you are my God whom I seek;
   for you my flesh pines and my soul thirsts
   like the earth, parched, lifeless and without water.

Thus have I gazed toward you in the sanctuary
    to see your power and your glory,
For your kindness is a greater good than life;
    my lips shall glorify you.

Thus will I bless you while I live;
    lifting up my hands, I will call upon your name.
As with the riches of a banquet shall my soul be satisfied,
    and with exultant lips my mouth shall praise you.

You are my help,
    and in the shadow of your wings I shout for joy.
My soul clings fast to you;
    your right hand upholds me.

From Psalm 63

Living the Word This Week

How can I make my life a gift for others in charity?

Offer a sacrifice this week for those around the world who are
persecuted for their faith in Christ.

September 10, 2023

Lectio Divina for the Twenty-Third Week in Ordinary Time

We begin our prayer:

In the name of the Father, and of the Son, and of the Holy Spirit. Amen.

O God, by whom we are redeemed and receive adoption,
look graciously upon your beloved sons and daughters,
that those who believe in Christ
may receive true freedom
and an everlasting inheritance.
Through our Lord Jesus Christ, your Son,
who lives and reigns with you in the unity of the Holy Spirit,
God, for ever and ever.

Collect, Twenty-Third Sunday in Ordinary Time

Reading (*Lectio*)

Read the following Scripture two or three times.

Matthew 18:15-20

> Jesus said to his disciples: "If your brother sins against you, go and tell him his fault between you and him alone. If he listens to you, you have won over your brother. If he does not listen, take one or two others along with you, so that 'every fact may be established on the testimony of two or three witnesses.' If he refuses to listen to them, tell the church. If he refuses to listen even to the church, then treat him as you would a Gentile or a tax collector. Amen, I say to you, whatever you bind on earth shall be bound in heaven, and whatever you loose on earth shall be loosed in heaven. Again, amen, I say to you, if two of you agree on earth about anything for which they are to pray, it shall be granted to them by my heavenly Father. For where two or three are gathered together in my name, there am I in the midst of them."

Meditation (*Meditatio*)

After the reading, take some time to reflect in silence on one or more of the following questions:

- What word or words in this passage caught your attention?
- What in this passage comforted you?
- What in this passage challenged you?

If practicing lectio divina *as a family or in a group, after the reflection time, invite the participants to share their responses.*

Prayer (*Oratio*)

Read the scripture passage one more time. Bring to the Lord the praise, petition, or thanksgiving that the Word inspires in you.

Contemplation (*Contemplatio*)

Read the Scripture again, followed by this reflection:

∼ What conversion of mind, heart, and life is the Lord asking of me?

_____

_____

_____

_____

∼ *If he listens to you, you have won over your brother.* How often have I spoken with others about what I believe? How have I accompanied those who are struggling with doubt?

_____

_____

_____

_____

~ *Every fact may be established on the testimony of two or three witnesses.* Whose faith witness have I found most compelling? How can I strengthen my own witness to what I believe?

_____

_____

_____

_____

~ *Again, amen, I say to you, if two of you agree on earth about anything for which they are to pray, it shall be granted to them by my heavenly Father.* What are my favorite ways to pray? How do I like to pray with others (my family, a small group, my parish community)?

_____

_____

_____

_____

~ *After a period of silent reflection and/or discussion, all recite the Lord's Prayer and the following:*

Closing Prayer

Come, let us sing joyfully to the LORD;
>   let us acclaim the rock of our salvation.
Let us come into his presence with thanksgiving;
>   let us joyfully sing psalms to him.

Come, let us bow down in worship;
>   let us kneel before the LORD who made us.
For he is our God,
>   and we are the people he shepherds, the flock he guides.

Oh, that today you would hear his voice:
>   "Harden not your hearts as at Meribah,
>   as in the day of Massah in the desert,
Where your fathers tempted me;
>   they tested me though they had seen my works."

From Psalm 95

Living the Word This Week

How can I make my life a gift for others in charity?

Attend Sunday Mass and be aware of Christ present in the gathered community.

September 17, 2023

Lectio Divina for the Twenty-Fourth Week in Ordinary Time

We begin our prayer:

In the name of the Father, and of the Son, and of the Holy Spirit. Amen.

Look upon us, O God,
Creator and ruler of all things,
and, that we may feel the working of your mercy,
grant that we may serve you with all our heart.
Through our Lord Jesus Christ, your Son,
who lives and reigns with you in the unity of the Holy Spirit,
God, for ever and ever.

Collect, Twenty-Fourth Sunday in Ordinary Time

Reading (*Lectio*)

Read the following Scripture two or three times.

Matthew 18:21-35

Peter approached Jesus and asked him, "Lord, if my brother sins against me, how often must I forgive? As many as seven times?" Jesus answered, "I say to you, not seven times but seventy-seven times. That is why the kingdom of heaven may be likened to a king who decided to settle accounts with his servants. When he began the accounting, a debtor was brought before him who owed him a huge amount. Since he had no way of paying it back, his master ordered him to be sold, along with his wife, his children, and all his property, in payment of the debt. At that, the servant fell down, did him homage, and said, 'Be patient with me, and I will pay you back in full.' Moved with compassion the master of that servant let him go and forgave him the loan. When that servant had left, he found one of his fellow servants who owed him a much smaller amount. He seized him and started to choke him, demanding, 'Pay back what you owe.' Falling to his knees, his fellow servant begged him, 'Be patient with me, and I will pay you back.' But he refused. Instead, he had the fellow servant put in prison until he paid back the debt. Now when his fellow servants saw what had happened, they were deeply disturbed, and went to their master and reported the whole affair. His master summoned him and said to him, 'You wicked servant! I forgave you your entire debt because you begged me to. Should you not have had pity on your fellow servant, as I had pity on you?' Then in anger his master handed him over to the torturers until he should pay back the whole debt. So will my heavenly Father do to you, unless each of you forgives your brother from your heart."

Meditation (*Meditatio*)

After the reading, take some time to reflect in silence on one or more of the following questions:

- What word or words in this passage caught your attention?
- What in this passage comforted you?
- What in this passage challenged you?

If practicing lectio divina *as a family or in a group, after the reflection time, invite the participants to share their responses.*

Prayer (*Oratio*)

Read the scripture passage one more time. Bring to the Lord the praise, petition, or thanksgiving that the Word inspires in you.

Contemplation (*Contemplatio*)

Read the Scripture again, followed by this reflection:

✦ What conversion of mind, heart, and life is the Lord asking of me?

_____

_____

_____

_____

~ *Lord, if my brother sins against me, how often must I forgive?* Who do I need to forgive? From whom do I need to ask forgiveness?

_____

_____

_____

_____

~ *Be patient with me.* In what ways do I need to be more patient with those around me? In what ways do I need to be more patient with myself?

_____

_____

_____

_____

~ *Now when his fellow servants saw what had happened, they were deeply disturbed, and went to their master and reported the whole affair.* When have I spoken out about injustices that I see? When have I failed to speak out?

_____

_____

_____

_____

∿ *After a period of silent reflection and/or discussion, all recite the Lord's Prayer and the following:*

Closing Prayer

Bless the LORD, O my soul;
    and all my being, bless his holy name.
Bless the LORD, O my soul,
    and forget not all his benefits.

He pardons all your iniquities,
    heals all your ills.
He redeems your life from destruction,
    crowns you with kindness and compassion.

He will not always chide,
    nor does he keep his wrath forever.
Not according to our sins does he deal with us,
    nor does he requite us according to our crimes.

For as the heavens are high above the earth,
    so surpassing is his kindness toward those who fear him.
As far as the east is from the west,
    so far has he put our transgressions from us.

From Psalm 103

Living the Word This Week

How can I make my life a gift for others in charity?

Read *God's Gift of Forgiveness: A Pastoral Exhortation on the Sacrament of Penance and Reconciliation*: http://www.usccb.org/ prayer-and-worship/sacraments-and-sacramentals/penance/upload/ Penance-Statement-ENG.pdf

September 24, 2023

Lectio Divina for the Twenty-Fifth Sunday in Ordinary Time

We begin our prayer:

In the name of the Father, and of the Son, and of the Holy Spirit. Amen.

O God, who founded all the commands of your sacred Law
upon love of you and of our neighbor,
grant that, by keeping your precepts,
we may merit to attain eternal life.
Through our Lord Jesus Christ, your Son,
who lives and reigns with you in the unity of the Holy Spirit,
God, for ever and ever.

Collect, Twenty-Fifth Sunday in Ordinary Time

Reading (*Lectio*)

Read the following Scripture two or three times.

Matthew 20:1-16a

Jesus told his disciples this parable: "The kingdom of heaven is like a landowner who went out at dawn to hire laborers for his vineyard. After agreeing with them for the usual daily wage, he sent them into his vineyard. Going out about nine o'clock, the landowner saw others standing idle in the marketplace, and he said to them, 'You too go into my vineyard, and I will give you what is just.' So they went off. And he went out again around noon, and around three o'clock, and did likewise. Going out about five o'clock, the landowner found others standing around, and said to them, 'Why do you stand here idle all day?' They answered, 'Because no one has hired us.' He said to them, 'You too go into my vineyard.' When it was evening the owner of the vineyard said to his foreman, 'Summon the laborers and give them their pay, beginning with the last and ending with the first.' When those who had started about five o'clock came, each received the usual daily wage. So when the first came, they thought that they would receive more, but each of them also got the usual wage. And on receiving it they grumbled against the landowner, saying, 'These last ones worked only one hour, and you have made them equal to us, who bore the day's burden and the heat.' He said to one of them in reply, 'My friend, I am not cheating you. Did you not agree with me for the usual daily wage? Take what is yours and go. What if I wish to give this last one the same as you? Or am I not free to do as I wish with my own money? Are you envious because I am generous?' Thus, the last will be first, and the first will be last."

Meditation (*Meditatio*)

After the reading, take some time to reflect in silence on one or more of the following questions:

- What word or words in this passage caught your attention?
- What in this passage comforted you?
- What in this passage challenged you?

If practicing lectio divina *as a family or in a group, after the reflection time, invite the participants to share their responses.*

Prayer (*Oratio*)

Read the scripture passage one more time. Bring to the Lord the praise, petition, or thanksgiving that the Word inspires in you.

Contemplation (*Contemplatio*)

Read the Scripture again, followed by this reflection:

≈ What conversion of mind, heart, and life is the Lord asking of me?

≈ *The kingdom of heaven is like a landowner who went out at dawn to hire laborers for his vineyard.* How am I being called to labor for the Lord? How can I prepare my heart to hear and respond to the Lord's call?

_____

_____

_____

_____

≈ *Why do you stand here idle all day?* When have I failed to act as I should? How have I become lazy in my spiritual life?

_____

_____

_____

_____

≈ *Thus, the last will be first, and the first will be last.* Who in my community is seen as "last"? How can I reach out to the forgotten and marginalized?

_____

_____

_____

_____

~ After a period of silent reflection and/or discussion, all recite the Lord's Prayer and the following:

Closing Prayer

Every day will I bless you,
   and I will praise your name forever and ever.
Great is the LORD and highly to be praised;
   his greatness is unsearchable.

The LORD is gracious and merciful,
   slow to anger and of great kindness.
The LORD is good to all
   and compassionate toward all his works.

The LORD is just in all his ways
   and holy in all his works.
The LORD is near to all who call upon him,
   to all who call upon him in truth.

From Psalm 145

Living the Word This Week

How can I make my life a gift for others in charity?

Learn about social justice initiatives in your parish and diocese and consider prayerfully how you might participate,

October 1, 2023

Lectio Divina for the Twenty-Sixth Sunday in Ordinary Time

We begin our prayer:

In the name of the Father, and of the Son, and of the Holy Spirit. Amen.

O God, who manifest your almighty power
above all by pardoning and showing mercy,
bestow, we pray, your grace abundantly upon us
and make those hastening to attain your promises
heirs to the treasures of heaven.
Through our Lord Jesus Christ, your Son,
who lives and reigns with you in the unity of the Holy Spirit,
God, for ever and ever.

Collect, Twenty-Sixth Sunday in Ordinary Time

Reading (*Lectio*)

Read the following Scripture two or three times.

Matthew 21:28-32

> Jesus said to the chief priests and elders of the people: "What is your opinion? A man had two sons. He came to the first and said, 'Son, go out and work in the vineyard today.' He said in reply, 'I will not, ' but afterwards changed his mind and went. The man came to the other son and gave the same order. He said in reply, 'Yes, sir, 'but did not go. Which of the two did his father's will?" They answered, "The first." Jesus said to them, "Amen, I say to you, tax collectors and prostitutes are entering the kingdom of God before you. When John came to you in the way of righteousness, you did not believe him; but tax collectors and prostitutes did. Yet even when you saw that, you did not later change your minds and believe him."

Meditation (*Meditatio*)

After the reading, take some time to reflect in silence on one or more of the following questions:

- What word or words in this passage caught your attention?
- What in this passage comforted you?
- What in this passage challenged you?

If practicing lectio divina *as a family or in a group, after the reflection time, invite the participants to share their responses.*

Prayer (*Oratio*)

Read the scripture passage one more time. Bring to the Lord the praise, petition, or thanksgiving that the Word inspires in you.

Contemplation (*Contemplatio*)

Read the Scripture again, followed by this reflection:

What conversion of mind, heart, and life is the Lord asking of me?

What is your opinion? How does Church teaching inform my positions and opinions? How do I deal with people whose views differ from my own?

He said in reply, "I will not," but afterwards changed his mind and went. When have I experienced conversion? What parts of my life require change?

Which of the two did his father's will? What keeps me from following the Father's will? How can I be more faithful to God's call?

After a period of silent reflection and/or discussion, all recite the Lord's Prayer and the following:

Closing Prayer

Your ways, O Lord, make known to me;
    teach me your paths,
guide me in your truth and teach me,
    for you are God my savior.

Remember that your compassion, O LORD,
    and your love are from of old.
The sins of my youth and my frailties remember not;
    in your kindness remember me,
    because of your goodness, O LORD.

Good and upright is the LORD;
    thus he shows sinners the way.
He guides the humble to justice,
    and teaches the humble his way.

From Psalm 35

Living the Word This Week

How can I make my life a gift for others in charity?

Before going to sleep each night, take some time to reflect on your day: how you experienced God's presence during the day, and how you responded to God's call.

October 8, 2023

Lectio Divina for the Twenty-Seventh Week in Ordinary Time

We begin our prayer:

In the name of the Father, and of the Son, and of the Holy Spirit. Amen.

Almighty ever-living God,
who in the abundance of your kindness
surpass the merits and the desires of those who entreat you,
pour out your mercy upon us
to pardon what conscience dreads
and to give what prayer does not dare to ask.
Through our Lord Jesus Christ, your Son,
who lives and reigns with you in the unity of the Holy Spirit,
God, for ever and ever.

Collect, Twenty-Seventh Sunday in Ordinary Time

Reading (*Lectio*)

Read the following Scripture two or three times.

Matthew 21:33-43

Jesus said to the chief priests and the elders of the people: "Hear another parable. There was a landowner who planted a vineyard, put a hedge around it, dug a wine press in it, and built a tower. Then he leased it to tenants and went on a journey. When vintage time drew near, he sent his servants to the tenants to obtain his produce. But the tenants seized the servants and one they beat, another they killed, and a third they stoned. Again he sent other servants, more numerous than the first ones, but they treated them in the same way. Finally, he sent his son to them, thinking, 'They will respect my son.' But when the tenants saw the son, they said to one another, 'This is the heir. Come, let us kill him and acquire his inheritance.' They seized him, threw him out of the vineyard, and killed him. What will the owner of the vineyard do to those tenants when he comes?" They answered him, "He will put those wretched men to a wretched death and lease his vineyard to other tenants who will give him the produce at the proper times." Jesus said to them, "Did you never read in the Scriptures:

The stone that the builders rejected
*   has become the cornerstone;*
by the Lord has this been done,
*   and it is wonderful in our eyes?*

Therefore, I say to you, the kingdom of God will be taken away from you and given to a people that will produce its fruit."

Meditation (*Meditatio*)

After the reading, take some time to reflect in silence on one or more of the following questions:

- What word or words in this passage caught your attention?
- What in this passage comforted you?
- What in this passage challenged you?

If practicing lectio divina *as a family or in a group, after the reflection time, invite the participants to share their responses.*

Prayer (*Oratio*)

Read the scripture passage one more time. Bring to the Lord the praise, petition, or thanksgiving that the Word inspires in you.

Contemplation (*Contemplatio*)

Read the Scripture again, followed by this reflection:

≈ What conversion of mind, heart, and life is the Lord asking of me?

_____

_____

_____

_____

≈ *This is the heir.* What parts of my Catholic heritage are most precious to me? What can I do to preserve and share that heritage?

_____

_____

_____

_____

≈ *By the Lord has this been done,/ and it is wonderful in our eyes.* How have I seen the Lord active in my life this week? How can I give God praise for all he has done for me?

_____

_____

_____

_____

≈ *Therefore, I say to you, the kingdom of God will be taken away from you and given to a people that will produce its fruit.* What fruits has my life of faith produced? How can this fruit help build up the kingdom of God?

_____

_____

_____

_____

~ *After a period of silent reflection and/or discussion, all recite the Lord's Prayer and the following:*

Closing Prayer

A vine from Egypt you transplanted;
>   you drove away the nations and planted it.
It put forth its foliage to the Sea,
>   its shoots as far as the River.

Why have you broken down its walls,
>   so that every passer-by plucks its fruit,
The boar from the forest lays it waste,
>   and the beasts of the field feed upon it?

Once again, O Lord of hosts,
>   look down from heaven, and see;
take care of this vine,
>   and protect what your right hand has planted
>   the son of man whom you yourself made strong.

Then we will no more withdraw from you;
>   give us new life, and we will call upon your name.
O Lord, God of hosts, restore us;
>   if your face shine upon us, then we shall be saved.

From Psalm 80

Living the Word This Week

How can I make my life a gift for others in charity?

Before bed each night, review your day to discern how faithfully you followed the commandments and lived your faith and to recognize when God was present.

October 15, 2023

Lectio Divina for the Twenty-Eighth Sunday in Ordinary Time

We begin our prayer:

In the name of the Father, and of the Son, and of the Holy Spirit. Amen.

May your grace, O Lord, we pray,
at all times go before us and follow after
and make us always determined
to carry out good works.
Through our Lord Jesus Christ, your Son,
who lives and reigns with you in the unity of the Holy Spirit,
God, for ever and ever.

Collect, Twenty-Eighth Sunday in Ordinary Time

Reading (*Lectio*)

Read the following Scripture two or three times.

Matthew 22:1-14

Jesus again in reply spoke to the chief priests and elders of the people in parables, saying, "The kingdom of heaven may be likened to a king who gave a wedding feast for his son. He dispatched his servants to summon the invited guests to the feast, but they refused to come. A second time he sent other servants, saying, 'Tell those invited: "Behold, I have prepared my banquet, my calves and fattened cattle are killed, and everything is ready; come to the feast."'" Some ignored the invitation and went away, one to his farm, another to his business. The rest laid hold of his servants, mistreated them, and killed them. The king was enraged and sent his troops, destroyed those murderers, and burned their city. Then he said to his servants, 'The feast is ready, but those who were invited were not worthy to come. Go out, therefore, into the main roads and invite to the feast whomever you find.' The servants went out into the streets and gathered all they found, bad and good alike, and the hall was filled with guests. But when the king came in to meet the guests, he saw a man there not dressed in a wedding garment. The king said to him, 'My friend, how is it that you came in here without a wedding garment?' But he was reduced to silence. Then the king said to his attendants, 'Bind his hands and feet, and cast him into the darkness outside, where there will be wailing and grinding of teeth.' Many are invited, but few are chosen."

Meditation (*Meditatio*)

After the reading, take some time to reflect in silence on one or more of the following questions:

- What word or words in this passage caught your attention?
- What in this passage comforted you?
- What in this passage challenged you?

If practicing lectio divina *as a family or in a group, after the reflection time, invite the participants to share their responses.*

Prayer (*Oratio*)

Read the scripture passage one more time. Bring to the Lord the praise, petition, or thanksgiving that the Word inspires in you.

Contemplation (*Contemplatio*)

Read the Scripture again, followed by this reflection:

~ What conversion of mind, heart, and life is the Lord asking of me?

_____

_____

_____

_____

~ *He dispatched his servants to summon the invited guests to the feast, but they refused to come.* How have I experienced God's invitation to a life of faith? How have I responded to that invitation?

_____

_____

_____

_____

≈ *The feast is ready, but those who were invited were not worthy to come.*
How can I prepare myself to celebrate the Eucharistic banquet? How
can I grow in virtue?

_____

_____

_____

_____

≈ *But he was reduced to silence.* When have I been silent in the face of sin
and injustice? How can I best use my voice, especially on behalf of
the marginalized?

_____

_____

~ *After a period of silent reflection and/or discussion, all recite the Lord's Prayer and the following:*

Closing Prayer

The LORD is my shepherd; I shall not want.
    In verdant pastures he gives me repose;
beside restful waters he leads me;
    he refreshes my soul.

He guides me in right paths
    for his name's sake.
Even though I walk in the dark valley
    I fear no evil; for you are at my side
with your rod and your staff
    that give me courage.

You spread the table before me
    in the sight of my foes;
you anoint my head with oil;
    my cup overflows.

Only goodness and kindness follow me
    all the days of my life;
and I shall dwell in the house of the LORD
    for years to come.

From Psalm 23

Living the Word This Week

How can I make my life a gift for others in charity?

Invite someone to join you for Mass or a devotion or program at your church.

October 22, 2023

Lectio Divina for the Twenty-Ninth Sunday in Ordinary Time

We begin our prayer:

In the name of the Father, and of the Son, and of the Holy Spirit. Amen.

Almighty ever-living God,
grant that we may always conform our will to yours
and serve your majesty in sincerity of heart.
Through our Lord Jesus Christ, your Son,
who lives and reigns with you in the unity of the Holy Spirit,
God, for ever and ever.

Collect, Twenty-Ninth Sunday in Ordinary Time

Reading (*Lectio*)

Read the following Scripture two or three times.

Matthew 22:15-21

> The Pharisees went off and plotted how they might entrap Jesus
> in speech. They sent their disciples to him, with the Herodians,

saying, "Teacher, we know that you are a truthful man and that you teach the way of God in accordance with the truth. And you are not concerned with anyone's opinion, for you do not regard a person's status. Tell us, then, what is your opinion: Is it lawful to pay the census tax to Caesar or not?" Knowing their malice, Jesus said, "Why are you testing me, you hypocrites? Show me the coin that pays the census tax." Then they handed him the Roman coin. He said to them, "Whose image is this and whose inscription?" They replied, "Caesar's." At that he said to them, "Then repay to Caesar what belongs to Caesar and to God what belongs to God."

Meditation (*Meditatio*)

After the reading, take some time to reflect in silence on one or more of the following questions:

- What word or words in this passage caught your attention?
- What in this passage comforted you?
- What in this passage challenged you?

If practicing lectio divina *as a family or in a group, after the reflection time, invite the participants to share their responses.*

Prayer (*Oratio*)

Read the scripture passage one more time. Bring to the Lord the praise, petition, or thanksgiving that the Word inspires in you.

Contemplation (*Contemplatio*)

Read the Scripture again, followed by this reflection:

≈ What conversion of mind, heart, and life is the Lord asking of me?

_____

_____

_____

_____

≈ *The Pharisees went off and plotted how they might entrap Jesus in speech.* Is my speech (in person and on social media) true and kind? How can I moderate my speech to bring people closer to Christ?

_____

_____

_____

_____

≈ *You teach the way of God in accordance with the truth.* How have I learned about my faith? How am I continuing to learn?

_____

_____

_____

_____

~ *Then repay to Caesar what belongs to Caesar and to God what belongs to God. What role does my faith play in my life as a citizen? How can I be a better steward of all that God has given me?*

~ *After a period of silent reflection and/or discussion, all recite the Lord's Prayer and the following:*

Closing Prayer

Sing to the LORD a new song;
    sing to the LORD, all you lands.
Tell his glory among the nations;
    among all peoples, his wondrous deeds.

For great is the LORD and highly to be praised;
    awesome is he, beyond all gods.
For all the gods of the nations are things of nought,
    but the LORD made the heavens.

Give to the LORD, you families of nations,
    give to the LORD glory and praise;
give to the LORD the glory due his name!
    Bring gifts, and enter his courts.

Worship the LORD, in holy attire;
    tremble before him, all the earth;
say among the nations: The LORD is king,
    he governs the peoples with equity.

From Psalm 96

Living the Word This Week

How can I make my life a gift for others in charity?

Learn more about becoming a faithful citizen:
https://www.usccb.org/offices/justice-peace-human-development/
forming-consciences-faithful-citizenship

October 29, 2023

Lectio Divina for the Thirtieth Sunday in Ordinary Time

We begin our prayer:

In the name of the Father, and of the Son, and of the Holy Spirit. Amen.

Almighty ever-living God,
increase our faith, hope and charity,
and make us love what you command,
so that we may merit what you promise.
Through our Lord Jesus Christ, your Son,
who lives and reigns with you in the unity of the Holy Spirit,
God, for ever and ever.

Collect, Thirtieth Sunday in Ordinary Time

Reading (*Lectio*)

Read the following Scripture two or three times.

Matthew 22:34-40

> When the Pharisees heard that Jesus had silenced the Sadducees, they gathered together, and one of them, a scholar of the law tested him by asking, "Teacher, which commandment in the law is the greatest?" He said to him, "You shall love the Lord, your God, with all your heart, with all your soul, and with all your mind. This is the greatest and the first commandment. The second is like it: You shall love your neighbor as yourself. The whole law and the prophets depend on these two commandments."

Meditation (*Meditatio*)

After the reading, take some time to reflect in silence on one or more of the following questions:

- What word or words in this passage caught your attention?
- What in this passage comforted you?
- What in this passage challenged you?

If practicing lectio divina *as a family or in a group, after the reflection time, invite the participants to share their responses.*

Prayer (*Oratio*)

Read the scripture passage one more time. Bring to the Lord the praise, petition, or thanksgiving that the Word inspires in you.

Contemplation (*Contemplatio*)

Read the Scripture again, followed by this reflection:

≈ What conversion of mind, heart, and life is the Lord asking of me?

_____

_____

_____

_____

≈ *When the Pharisees heard that Jesus had silenced the Sadducees.* Whose voices are missing in public discourse? Whose voices do I fail to listen for?

_____

_____

_____

_____

≈ *Teacher, which commandment in the law is the greatest?* Which of God's commandments do I find the greatest challenge? Which of God's commandments do I find the greatest joy?

_____

_____

∾ *You shall love your neighbor as yourself.* Who is my neighbor? How do I express my love for my neighbor?

_____

_____

_____

_____

∾ *After a period of silent reflection and/or discussion, all recite the Lord's Prayer and the following:*

Closing Prayer

I love you, O LORD, my strength,
  O LORD, my rock, my fortress, my deliverer.

My God, my rock of refuge,
  my shield, the horn of my salvation, my stronghold!
Praised be the LORD, I exclaim,
  and I am safe from my enemies.

The LORD lives and blessed be my rock!
  Extolled be God my savior.
You who gave great victories to your king
  and showed kindness to your anointed.

From Psalm 18

Living the Word This Week

How can I make my life a gift for others in charity?

Join the issue advocacy network of your diocese or state Catholic
conference.

November 1, 2023

Lectio Divina for the Solemnity of All Saints

We begin our prayer:

In the name of the Father, and of the Son, and of the Holy Spirit. Amen.

Almighty ever-living God,
by whose gift we venerate in one celebration
the merits of all the Saints,
bestow on us, we pray,
through the prayers of so many intercessors,
an abundance of the reconciliation with you
for which we earnestly long.
Through our Lord Jesus Christ, your Son,
who lives and reigns with you in the unity of the Holy Spirit,
God, for ever and ever.

Collect, Solemnity of All Saints

Reading (*Lectio*)

Read the following Scripture two or three times.

Matthew 5:1-12a

When Jesus saw the crowds, he went up the mountain, and after he had sat down, his disciples came to him. He began to teach them, saying:

"Blessed are the poor in spirit,
　　for theirs is the Kingdom of heaven.
Blessed are they who mourn,
　　for they will be comforted.
Blessed are the meek,
　　for they will inherit the land.
Blessed are they who hunger and thirst for righteousness,
　　for they will be satisfied.
Blessed are the merciful,
　　for they will be shown mercy.
Blessed are the clean of heart,
　　for they will see God.
Blessed are the peacemakers,
　　for they will be called children of God.
Blessed are they who are persecuted for the sake of righteousness,
　　for theirs is the Kingdom of heaven.
Blessed are you when they insult you and persecute you
　　and utter every kind of evil against you falsely because of me.
Rejoice and be glad,
　　for your reward will be great in heaven."

Meditation (*Meditatio*)

After the reading, take some time to reflect in silence on one or more of the following questions:

- What word or words in this passage caught your attention?
- What in this passage comforted you?
- What in this passage challenged you?

If practicing lectio divina *as a family or in a group, after the reflection time, invite the participants to share their responses.*

Prayer (*Oratio*)

Read the scripture passage one more time. Bring to the Lord the praise, petition, or thanksgiving that the Word inspires in you.

Contemplation (*Contemplatio*)

Read the Scripture again, followed by this reflection:

≈ What conversion of mind, heart, and life is the Lord asking of me?

_____

_____

_____

_____

≈ *Blessed are they who hunger and thirst for righteousness,/ for they will be satisfied.* How can I live more righteously? How does God satisfy the hungers of my heart?

_____

_____

_____

_____

≈ *Blessed are the clean of heart,/ for they will see God.* What areas of impurity in my life need to be cleansed? How can I set my heart more fully on God?

_____

_____

_____

_____

≈ *Blessed are you when they insult you and persecute you and utter every kind of evil against you falsely because of me.* When have I been mocked or challenged because of my faith? When have I contributed to the mocking of others?

_____

_____

After a period of silent reflection and/or discussion, all recite the Lord's Prayer and the following:

Closing Prayer

The LORD's are the earth and its fullness;
    the world and those who dwell in it.
For he founded it upon the seas
    and established it upon the rivers.

Who can ascend the mountain of the LORD?
    or who may stand in his holy place?
One whose hands are sinless, whose heart is clean,
    who desires not what is vain.

He shall receive a blessing from the LORD,
    a reward from God his savior.
Such is the race that seeks him,
    that seeks the face of the God of Jacob.

From Psalm 24

Living the Word This Week

How can I make my life a gift for others in charity?

Learn more about Christians around the world who are persecuted for their faith: http://www.usccb.org/issues-and-action/religious-liberty/international-religious-freedom.cfm.

November 5, 2023

Lectio Divina for the Thirty-First Sunday in Ordinary Time

We begin our prayer:

In the name of the Father, and of the Son, and of the Holy Spirit. Amen.

Almighty and merciful God,
by whose gift your faithful offer you
right and praiseworthy service,
grant, we pray,
that we may hasten without stumbling
to receive the things you have promised.
Through our Lord Jesus Christ, your Son,
who lives and reigns with you in the unity of the Holy Spirit,
God, for ever and ever.

Collect, Thirty-First Sunday in Ordinary Time

Reading (*Lectio*)

Read the following Scripture two or three times.

Matthew 23:1-12

Jesus spoke to the crowds and to his disciples, saying, "The scribes and the Pharisees have taken their seat on the chair of Moses. Therefore, do and observe all things whatsoever they tell you, but do not follow their example. For they preach but they do not practice. They tie up heavy burdens hard to carry and lay them on people's shoulders, but they will not lift a finger to move them. All their works are performed to be seen. They widen their phylacteries and lengthen their tassels. They love places of honor at banquets, seats of honor in synagogues, greetings in marketplaces, and the salutation 'Rabbi.' As for you, do not be called 'Rabbi.' You have but one teacher, and you are all brothers. Call no one on earth your father; you have but one Father in heaven. Do not be called 'Master'; you have but one master, the Christ. The greatest among you must be your servant. Whoever exalts himself will be humbled; but whoever humbles himself will be exalted."

Meditation (*Meditatio*)

After the reading, take some time to reflect in silence on one or more of the following questions:

- What word or words in this passage caught your attention?
- What in this passage comforted you?
- What in this passage challenged you?

If practicing lectio divina *as a family or in a group, after the reflection time, invite the participants to share their responses.*

Prayer (*Oratio*)

Read the scripture passage one more time. Bring to the Lord the praise, petition, or thanksgiving that the Word inspires in you.

Contemplation (*Contemplatio*)

Read the Scripture again, followed by this reflection:

∾ What conversion of mind, heart, and life is the Lord asking of me?

_____

_____

_____

_____

∾ *For they preach but they do not practice.* When have I failed to live according to my beliefs? How do my actions support and demonstrate my faith?

_____

_____

_____

_____

~ *They tie up heavy burdens hard to carry and lay them on people's shoulders, but they will not lift a finger to move them.* How have my actions added to the burdens that others must carry? How have I failed to assist others in carrying their burdens?

_____

_____

_____

_____

~ *The greatest among you must be your servant.* How can I offer loving service to those around me? How can I develop a servant's heart?

_____

_____

_____

_____

~ *After a period of silent reflection and/or discussion, all recite the Lord's Prayer and the following:*

Closing Prayer

O LORD, my heart is not proud,
    nor are my eyes haughty;
I busy not myself with great things,
    nor with things too sublime for me.

Nay rather, I have stilled and quieted
    my soul like a weaned child.
Like a weaned child on its mother's lap,
    so is my soul within me.

O Israel, hope in the LORD,
    both now and forever.

From Psalm 131

Living the Word This Week

How can I make my life a gift for others in charity?

Learn more about putting the two feet of love in action:
https://www.usccb.org/beliefs-and-teachings/what-we-believe/
catholic-social-teaching/two-feet-of-love-in-action

November 12, 2023

Lectio Divina for the Thirty-Second Sunday in Ordinary Time

We begin our prayer:

In the name of the Father, and of the Son, and of the Holy Spirit. Amen.

Almighty and merciful God,
graciously keep from us all adversity,
so that, unhindered in mind and body alike,
we may pursue in freedom of heart
the things that are yours.
Through our Lord Jesus Christ, your Son,
who lives and reigns with you in the unity of the Holy Spirit,
God, for ever and ever.

Collect, Thirty-Second Sunday in Ordinary Time

Reading (*Lectio*)

Read the following Scripture two or three times.

Matthew 25:1-13

Jesus told his disciples this parable: "The kingdom of heaven will be like ten virgins who took their lamps and went out to meet the bridegroom. Five of them were foolish and five were wise. The foolish ones, when taking their lamps, brought no oil with them, but the wise brought flasks of oil with their lamps. Since the bridegroom was long delayed, they all became drowsy and fell asleep. At midnight, there was a cry, 'Behold, the bridegroom! Come out to meet him!' Then all those virgins got up and trimmed their lamps. The foolish ones said to the wise, 'Give us some of your oil, for our lamps are going out.' But the wise ones replied, 'No, for there may not be enough for us and you. Go instead to the merchants and buy some for yourselves.' While they went off to buy it, the bridegroom came and those who were ready went into the wedding feast with him. Then the door was locked. Afterwards the other virgins came and said, 'Lord, Lord, open the door for us!' But he said in reply, 'Amen, I say to you, I do not know you.' Therefore, stay awake, for you know neither the day nor the hour."

Meditation (*Meditatio*)

After the reading, take some time to reflect in silence on one or more of the following questions:

- What word or words in this passage caught your attention?
- What in this passage comforted you?
- What in this passage challenged you?

If practicing lectio divina *as a family or in a group, after the reflection time, invite the participants to share their responses.*

Prayer (*Oratio*)

Read the scripture passage one more time. Bring to the Lord the praise, petition, or thanksgiving that the Word inspires in you.

Contemplation (*Contemplatio*)

Read the Scripture again, followed by this reflection:

≈ What conversion of mind, heart, and life is the Lord asking of me?

_____

_____

_____

_____

≈ *Behold, the bridegroom! Come out to meet him!* Where have I met the Lord? How can I help others meet Jesus?

_____

_____

_____

_____

≈ *No, for there may not be enough for us and you.* How do I decide if I have "enough"? How can I grow in generosity?

_____

_____

_____

_____

≈ *Those who were ready went into the wedding feast with him.* How do I prepare to celebrate the Eucharistic banquet? How can I continue to grow closer to Jesus in the Eucharist?

_____

_____

_____

_____

≈ *After a period of silent reflection and/or discussion, all recite the Lord's Prayer and the following:*

Closing Prayer

O God, you are my God whom I seek;
    for you my flesh pines and my soul thirsts
    like the earth, parched, lifeless and without water.

Thus have I gazed toward you in the sanctuary
    to see your power and your glory,
For your kindness is a greater good than life;
    my lips shall glorify you.

Thus will I bless you while I live;
    lifting up my hands, I will call upon your name.
As with the riches of a banquet shall my soul be satisfied,
    and with exultant lips my mouth shall praise you.

I will remember you upon my couch,
    and through the night-watches I will meditate on you:
You are my help,
    and in the shadow of your wings I shout for joy.

From Psalm 63

Living the Word This Week

How can I make my life a gift for others in charity?

Read Part II of *The Mystery of the Eucharist in the Life of the Church*:
https://www.usccb.org/resources/7-703%20The%20Mystery%20
of%20Eucharist,%20for%20RE-UPLOAD,%20JANUARY%202022.pdf

November 19, 2023

Lectio Divina for the Thirty-Third Sunday in Ordinary Time

We begin our prayer:

In the name of the Father, and of the Son, and of the Holy Spirit. Amen.

Grant us, we pray, O Lord our God,
the constant gladness of being devoted to you,
for it is full and lasting happiness
to serve with constancy
the author of all that is good.
Through our Lord Jesus Christ, your Son,
who lives and reigns with you in the unity of the Holy Spirit,
God, for ever and ever.

Collect, Thirty-Third Sunday in Ordinary Time

Reading (*Lectio*)

Read the following Scripture two or three times.

Matthew 25:14-30

Jesus told his disciples this parable: "A man going on a journey called in his servants and entrusted his possessions to them. To one he gave five talents; to another, two; to a third, one--to each according to his ability. Then he went away. Immediately the one who received five talents went and traded with them, and made another five. Likewise, the one who received two made another two. But the man who received one went off and dug a hole in the ground and buried his master's money.

"After a long time the master of those servants came back and settled accounts with them. The one who had received five talents came forward bringing the additional five. He said, 'Master, you gave me five talents. See, I have made five more.' His master said to him, 'Well done, my good and faithful servant. Since you were faithful in small matters, I will give you great responsibilities. Come, share your master's joy.' Then the one who had received two talents also came forward and said, 'Master, you gave me two talents. See, I have made two more.' His master said to him, 'Well done, my good and faithful servant. Since you were faithful in small matters, I will give you great responsibilities. Come, share your master's joy.' Then the one who had received the one talent came forward and said, 'Master, I knew you were a demanding person, harvesting where you did not plant and gathering where you did not scatter; so out of fear I went off and buried your talent in the ground. Here it is back.' His master said to him in reply, 'You wicked, lazy servant! So you knew that I harvest where I did not plant and gather where I did not scatter? Should you not then have put my money in the bank so that I could have got it back with interest on my return? Now then! Take the talent from him and give it to the one with ten. For to everyone who has, more will be given and he will grow rich; but from the one who has not, even what he has will be taken away. And throw this useless servant into the darkness outside, where there will be wailing and grinding of teeth.'"

Meditation (*Meditatio*)

After the reading, take some time to reflect in silence on one or more of the following questions:

- What word or words in this passage caught your attention?
- What in this passage comforted you?
- What in this passage challenged you?

If practicing lectio divina *as a family or in a group, after the reflection time, invite the participants to share their responses.*

Prayer (*Oratio*)

Read the scripture passage one more time. Bring to the Lord the praise, petition, or thanksgiving that the Word inspires in you.

Contemplation (*Contemplatio*)

Read the Scripture again, followed by this reflection:

≈ What conversion of mind, heart, and life is the Lord asking of me?

_____

_____

_____

_____

≈ *But the man who received one went off and dug a hole in the ground and buried his master's money.* What have I done to develop my God-given gifts? When have I hidden my faith instead of giving witness?

_____

_____

_____

_____

≈ *Since you were faithful in small matters, I will give you great responsibilities.* What responsibilities has God given me? How does faithfully fulfilling my responsibilities give witness to my faith?

_____

_____

_____

_____

~ *Come, share your master's joy.* How have I experienced God's holy joy this week? How can I share that joy with others?

_____

_____

_____

_____

~ *After a period of silent reflection and/or discussion, all recite the Lord's Prayer and the following:*

Closing Prayer

Blessed are you who fear the LORD,
    who walk in his ways!
For you shall eat the fruit of your handiwork;
    blessed shall you be, and favored.

Your wife shall be like a fruitful vine
    in the recesses of your home;
Your children like olive plants
    around your table.

Behold, thus is the man blessed
    who fears the LORD.
The LORD bless you from Zion:
    may you see the prosperity of Jerusalem
    all the days of your life.

From Psalm 128

Living the Word This Week

How can I make my life a gift for others in charity?

Research volunteer opportunities in your parish, diocese, or community and put your talents to work for the common good.

November 26, 2023

Lectio Divina for the Solemnity of Our Lord Jesus Christ, King of the Universe

We begin our prayer:

In the name of the Father, and of the Son, and of the Holy Spirit. Amen.

Almighty ever-living God,
whose will is to restore all things
in your beloved Son, the King of the universe,
grant, we pray,
that the whole creation, set free from slavery,
may render your majesty service
and ceaselessly proclaim your praise.
Through our Lord Jesus Christ, your Son,
who lives and reigns with you in the unity of the Holy Spirit,
God, for ever and ever.

Collect, Solemnity of Our Lord Jesus Christ, King of the Universe

Reading (*Lectio*)

Read the following Scripture two or three times.

Matthew 25:31-46

Jesus said to his disciples: "When the Son of Man comes in his glory, and all the angels with him, he will sit upon his glorious throne, and all the nations will be assembled before him. And he will separate them one from another, as a shepherd separates the sheep from the goats. He will place the sheep on his right and the goats on his left. Then the king will say to those on his right, 'Come, you who are blessed by my Father. Inherit the kingdom prepared for you from the foundation of the world. For I was hungry and you gave me food, I was thirsty and you gave me drink, a stranger and you welcomed me, naked and you clothed me, ill and you cared for me, in prison and you visited me.' Then the righteous will answer him and say, 'Lord, when did we see you hungry and feed you, or thirsty and give you drink? When did we see you a stranger and welcome you, or naked and clothe you? When did we see you ill or in prison, and visit you?' And the king will say to them in reply, 'Amen, I say to you, whatever you did for one of the least brothers of mine, you did for me.' Then he will say to those on his left, 'Depart from me, you accursed, into the eternal fire prepared for the devil and his angels. For I was hungry and you gave me no food, I was thirsty and you gave me no drink, a stranger and you gave me no welcome, naked and you gave me no clothing, ill and in prison, and you did not care for me.' Then they will answer and say, 'Lord, when did we see you hungry or thirsty or a stranger or naked or ill or in prison, and not minister to your needs?' He will answer them, 'Amen, I say to you, what you did not do for one of these least ones, you did not do for me.' And these will go off to eternal punishment, but the righteous to eternal life."

Meditation (*Meditatio*)

After the reading, take some time to reflect in silence on one or more of the following questions:

- What word or words in this passage caught your attention?
- What in this passage comforted you?
- What in this passage challenged you?

If practicing lectio divina *as a family or in a group, after the reflection time, invite the participants to share their responses.*

Prayer (*Oratio*)

Read the scripture passage one more time. Bring to the Lord the praise, petition, or thanksgiving that the Word inspires in you.

Contemplation (*Contemplatio*)

Read the Scripture again, followed by this reflection:

≈ What conversion of mind, heart, and life is the Lord asking of me?

~ *And he will separate them one from another, as a shepherd separates the sheep from the goats.* How have I been a force for division rather than unity? How do I discern ways to pursue what is good and avoid what is evil?

_____

_____

_____

_____

~ *Amen, I say to you, whatever you did for one of the least brothers of mine, you did for me.* What acts of kindness and mercy have I performed this week? What opportunities for kindness and mercy have I let slip away?

_____

_____

_____

_____

~ *And these will go off to eternal punishment, but the righteous to eternal life.* How am I preparing my soul to meet the Lord on the day of judgment? How can I increase my longing to live with God forever?

_____

_____

～ After a period of silent reflection and/or discussion, all recite the Lord's Prayer and the following:

Closing Prayer

The Lord is my shepherd; I shall not want.
　　In verdant pastures he gives me repose.

Beside restful waters he leads me;
　　he refreshes my soul.
He guides me in right paths
　　for his name's sake.

You spread the table before me
　　in the sight of my foes;
you anoint my head with oil;
　　my cup overflows.

Only goodness and kindness follow me
　　all the days of my life;
and I shall dwell in the house of the Lord
　　for years to come.

From Psalm 23

Living the Word This Week

How can I make my life a gift for others in charity?

Commit to performing the corporal works of mercy in the
coming month(s): http://www.usccb.org/beliefs-and-teachings/
how-we-teach/new-evangelization/jubilee-of-mercy/
the-corporal-works-of-mercy.cfm

CPSIA information can be obtained
at www.ICGtesting.com
Printed in the USA
JSHW040102110922
30263JS00002B/2